Grundmann · Schairer · Weinzierl

THE CONFLICT IN NORTHERN IRELAND

Bayerischer Schulbuch-Verlag · München

bsv Englisch für den Sekundarbereich II
herausgegeben von Klaus Weinzierl

Der Titel wurde in der Ausstellung „Drei Drucker in Irland"
(München, Neue Sammlung, November 1976)
aus Holzlettern der Druckerei Corrigan & Wilson, Dublin,
von den Autoren gesetzt und gedruckt.
Many thanks to Gerd Fleischmann and his team!
Thanks to Eve Pennell, Liz Goldmann and
John G. Harper for reading and suggestions.

1988
4. Auflage, 2. Nachdruck
© Bayerischer Schulbuch-Verlag
Hubertusstraße 4, 8000 München 19
Gesamtherstellung: Ernst Kieser GmbH, 8902 Neusäß
ISBN 3-7627-5057-2

Vorwort

Das vorliegende Arbeitsbuch "The Conflict in Northern Ireland" ist entwickelt worden auf der Grundlage mehrjähriger Unterrichtspraxis an einer Münchner Kollegstufen-Versuchsschule.

Es ist geeignet für den Englischunterricht in der reformierten Oberstufe des Gymnasiums (11. Klasse, Grund- und Leistungskurs), in Schularten der Sekundarstufe II, soweit vergleichbare Voraussetzungen in der Fremdsprache gegeben sind, und für projektorientierte Kurse und Übungen im Rahmen eines Grundstudiums Anglistik.

Ausgangspunkt der Arbeit des Autorenteams war ein täglich erfahrbares Dilemma des Englischlehrers: einerseits setzen die Lehrpläne der reformierten Oberstufe anspruchsvolle Lernziele, andererseits aber hat der Englischlehrer nicht in dem wünschenswerten Maß geeignete Unterrichtsmaterialien zur Verfügung. Der überwiegende Teil der bisher veröffentlichten Kursmaterialien ist strenggenommen immer noch konzipiert als Sammlung von prüfungsorientierten Textaufgaben.

Das vorliegende Arbeitsbuch ist entwickelt worden als Unterrichtsprogramm für einen themenbestimmten, lernzielorientierten Englischunterricht. Die prüfungsorientierte Textaufgabe ist darin nicht Lerninhalt des Unterrichts, sondern markiert den Abschluß bestimmter Phasen des Lernprozesses.

Das Arbeitsbuch ist gekennzeichnet durch eine große Vielfalt von Textsorten, einen hohen Anteil visueller Materialien, die nicht illustratives Beiwerk, sondern integriertes Arbeitsmaterial sind, und durch abwechslungsreiche Arbeitsformen, bei denen situationsbezogene Schreib- und Sprechakte im Vordergrund stehen. Der Bausteincharakter des Buches, sowohl bei den Materialien als auch bei den Arbeitsaufträgen, ermöglicht einen breiten Spielraum für die Auswahl und Differenzierung entsprechend der jeweiligen Kurssituation.

In der Lehrerhandreichung zum Arbeitsbuch werden drei Kursprogramme auf drei verschiedenen Lernniveaus exemplarisch zusammengestellt.

Das Arbeitsbuch will einen Beitrag zu einem Englischunterricht leisten, der auf den drei Ebenen Inhalt, Sprache und Interaktion das Lernziel kommunikative Kompetenz ernstnimmt, nicht nur in der Lehrplanpräambel, sondern gerade in der täglichen Unterrichtspraxis.

Die Wahl des Nordirlandkonflikts als Inhalt eines solchen Arbeitsbuches erfolgte nicht wegen seiner vordergründigen Aktualität. Vielmehr können an diesem Konflikt exemplarisch komplexe geschichtliche, gesellschaftliche und politische Zusammenhänge einsichtig gemacht werden ("800 years of Anglo-Irish history"). Wie kaum ein anderes Thema ist dieser Konflikt geeignet, stereotype Betrachtungsmuster (hier z. B. mittelalterlicher Religionskrieg) zu problematisieren und damit verbundene Vorurteile abzubauen. Trotz ständiger Nachrichtenflut, meist über aktuelle, spektakuläre Ereignisse, ist der Informationsstand über die Ursachen und Hintergründe völlig unzureichend.

Neben den wirtschaftlichen Problemen und der sich verschärfenden Rassenfrage rührt der Nordirlandkonflikt an den politischen Nerv Großbritanniens. Eine Lösung selbst in Ansätzen ist nicht in Sicht.

Die sorgfältige Materialauswahl und die Aufbereitung vermitteln inhaltlich und sprachlich den gegenwärtigen Stand einer kritischen, öffentlichen Diskussion in Großbritannien, nicht mehr und nicht weniger, und ermöglichen dem Schüler und Studenten, zu einem selbständigen Urteil zu gelangen.

München, Mai 1978

Rainer Grundmann
Ditz Schairer
Klaus Weinzierl

Beim Nachdruck des Arbeitsbuches wurde diesmal die "Chronology" (S. 114 ff.) aktualisiert. Die Grundprobleme in Nordirland haben sich 1988 noch nicht verändert. Eine politische Lösung ist auch nach dem "Anglo-Irish Agreement" zwischen Dublin und London nicht in Sicht. Aber die Zahl der Opfer in dieser mörderischen Auseinandersetzung in einem Teil Europas steigt weiter. Zwischen August 1969 und

März 1988 sind 2645 Menschen in Nordirland getötet worden, in einem Land, das so groß ist wie Oberbayern und so viele Einwohner hat wie München und Umgebung.

München, Juni 1988
Klaus Weinzierl, Ditz Schairer

3

Inhalt

Systematischer Aufbau des Arbeitsbuches

Contents	Texts and materials (course material)	Extra material	What you have to do (oral and written work)	Feedback: Oral and written exercises
Part 1: Who is fighting whom – what is the fight about				
1. What do you know about the conflict? (p. 12–15)	1. Photograph (Catholic boy from Bogside) 2. Questionnaire 3. Cartoon 4. Two photographs of Bogside Battle		1. Guided conversation 3. Answering a questionnaire 4. Guided discussion	2. Summary of a conversation
2. The conflict seen by a young Protestant from Belfast (p. 16–21)	Text: "What 7 years of Belfast violence have done to Alcwyn McKee"		1. Phrasal verbs 2. Structured vocabulary 3. Questions on the text	4. "How to interview people" (teamwork)
3. The immediate causes of the conflict (p. 22–27)	1. Text: "Who is fighting whom? What is the fight about?" 2. Graphs		1. Structured vocabulary 2. Version 3. Preparing statements for short speeches (teamwork)	4. Statements (short speeches and – optional – debate) in class

5

Contents	Texts and materials (course material)	Extra material	What you have to do (oral and written work)	Feedback: Oral and written exercises
4. Introducing a long story (p. 28–29)	Cartoon "Putting the clock back"		1. Analysing a cartoon	2. Written analysis (summing up the discussion of the cartoon)

Part 2: A long story in Ireland. 800 years of Anglo-Irish history

Contents	Texts and materials (course material)	Extra material	What you have to do (oral and written work)	Feedback: Oral and written exercises
1. The first English conquest (p. 32–33)	Text: "1171. The first English conquest of Ireland"		1. Questions on the text	2. Guided comment (on a text by C. M. Claxton)
2. British settlement in Ireland 16th–18th century (p. 34–39)	1. Text: "16th–17th cent. The Tudor Conquest" 2. Text: "1649 The Cromwellian settlement" 3. Text: "The Battle of the Boyne 1690" 4. Map: The British Conquest of Ireland		1. Diagram fill-in "The transfer of land ownership in Ireland 1603–1778" Or: Information by teacher and listening comprehension	2. Summary "The making of a colony"

Contents	Texts and materials (course material)	Extra material	What you have to do (oral and written work)	Feedback: Oral and written exercises
3. The United Irishmen's Insurrection (p. 40—47)	1. Text: "1798. The United Irishmen's Insurrection" 2. Illustrating map	*Ireland 1798 – North America 1776. A comparison*	1. Questions on the text *1. Guided analysis (teamwork)* *2. Summary (comparison Ireland—USA)* Or: Information by teacher and listening comprehension	2. Comment (on a text by C. M. Claxton)
4. The Great Famine (p. 48—52)	Text: "1840s: The Great Famine"	*Irish literature: Brendan Kennelly "My Dark Fathers":* 1. Text (poem) 2. Author's comment "Famine"	1. Guided analysis (questions) *Understanding the poem (questions)*	2. Summary "The Great Famine in Ireland"
5. The Easter Rising (p. 53—61)	Text: "Dublin 1916. The Easter Rising"	*1. Proclamation of the Irish Republic 1916* *2. Irish literature: William Butler Yeats "Easter 1916": Introductory note Text (poem)*	1. Guided analysis (teamwork) *1. Questions on the text* *2. Understanding the poem* Or: Information by teacher or short speeches in class and listening comprehension	2. Comment "The Easter Rising 1916 . . ."

Contents	Texts and materials (course material)	Extra material	What you have to do (oral and written work)	Feedback: Oral and written exercises
6. The Partition of Ireland (p. 62–70) 	1. Text: "1920 Partition" 2. Graphs and maps	"Gerrymandering" 1. Definition 2. Report Text 3. Text Diagram	1. Guided analysis (questions, maps, statistics) (teamwork) *Prepare a speech (teamwork) "How the Protestants in Ulster managed to construct a Protestant state . . ."*	2. Essay "The partition of Ireland in 1920"

Part 3: The troubles in Northern Ireland

Contents	Texts and materials (course material)	Extra material	What you have to do (oral and written work)	Feedback: Oral and written exercises
1. The 1960s: Why the troubles began (p. 72–77) 	Text: "The 1960s: Why the troubles began"		1. Questions on the text 3. Version 5. Text and style	2. Summary "Why did the 'troubles' in Northern Ireland begin in the late 1960s?" 4. Comment
2. British policy in Ulster 1969–1972: Military intervention (p. 78–81) 	1. Text: "August 1969 – January 1972 Military intervention: British troops move in" 2. Graph The violent pattern of Ulster 1969–72		1. Questions an the text	2. Guided analysis "The Army's job in Ulster August 1969 – January 1972"

8

Contents	Texts and materials (course material)	Extra material	What you have to do (oral and written work)	Feedback: Oral and written exercises
3. British policy in Ulster 1972–1978: Direct Rule (p. 82–94) 	1. Cartoon 2. Text: "1972–1977 Direct Rule: The problems unsolved" 3. Graph The violent pattern of Ulster 1972–1975	*Text: Ulster 1972–1977 "The failure of reconciliation".*	1. Analysing a cartoon 2. Version 3. Questions on the text *Comment (teamwork) Short speeches: "Why reconciliation has failed in Ulster so far"*	4. Guided comment "How far does the Ulster pattern of violence shown in the graph support the author's view …?" *Comprehension piece 1 "How the IRA gained a sniper"* *Comprehension piece 2 "Why the Army is there"*

Part 4: Solutions

1. What can be done? (p. 96–116) 	1. Text: "Should we get out?" 2. Text: "Civil war if we quit Ulster!" 3. Text: "Why Britain should leave Ulster" 4. Opinion poll June 1981 5. Text: "But there isn't any easy solution"	1. *Texts: Should we get out? Six 'letters to the editor'* 2. *"800 years of Anglo-Irish history"–chronology*	1. Guided analysis (questions) 2. Version Guided analysis (questions) Writing a news article 4. Version Guided analysis (questions) 1. *"Write a letter to the editor!"* 6. Discussion "Is there a way to an acceptable solution in N.I. now?"	3. Discussion (based on:) short statements (teamwork) 5. Guided comment "Three views on a British withdrawal from Northern Ireland" *Comprehension piece 3 "The releasing of Northern Ireland"*

Who whom? What about?

REMEMBER 1690

Part 1:
Who is fighting whom – what is the fight about

What do you know about the conflict?

What you have to do

Guided conversation
Summary (of a conversation)
Answering a questionnaire
Guided discussion
(photographs, cartoon)

Guided conversation

Let's talk about the photograph on the cover. The following questions are a guiding line.

This boy is said to be about eight.
Is that surprising to you?
Have you come across a photograph like that before?
What are the most striking features in the picture?
Do the petrol bomb in the boy's right hand and the gas mask over his face have anything to do with the badge on his jacket?
Look at the boy's hands. What is he waiting for?
Do you think the boy is about to defend himself?
Is he going to attack somebody or something?
Where is the other side?

Summary of a conversation

Summarize the conversation (in about 80–100 words).

The following phrases may be of some help to you:

– this photograph was taken with a 300 mm telephoto lens
– *in* this photograph you see . . .
– on the left/on the left side/on the left-hand side
– in the background
– top left, bottom left,/ . . . right

– I'm not quite sure, but . . .
– to me it seems to be . . .
– you can't tell from this photo if . . . /you can tell . . .
– I guess/I think . . .
– *to* my mind/*in* my opinion . . .
– I come to the conclusion that . . .

Questionnaire:
What do you know about Ireland?

Answer the following questions

1. Is Northern Ireland ("Ulster") smaller or bigger than Bavaria?
2. How many people live in Northern Ireland?
3. How big is the population of the Republic of Ireland ("Eire")?

4. What percentage of the population of Northern Ireland is Catholic and what percentage Protestant?
5. What is the ratio between Protestants and Catholics in the Republic of Ireland?
6. What is the political status of Northern Ireland:
   a) an independent state?
   b) part of the Republic of Ireland?
   c) integrated part of the United Kingdom (Great Britain) like Scotland and Wales?
7. How many people have been killed in Northern Ireland since the troubles began in 1969?
8. What kind of connections, if any, exist between the Federal Republic of Germany and Northern Ireland?

Guided discussion

1. Have a look at the two photographs, taken during riots in Londonderry in 1969.
   There are two sides involved in a fight. Who is fighting whom?
2. Now have a look at the cartoon.
   Who is fighting whom?
   What does the cartoon tell us about the two communities in Northern Ireland?
   Is the background in the cartoon of any importance?

3. The photographs don't show any victims.
   What victims does the cartoon show?
   What is the cartoonist's message?
4. Let's sum up:
   What do the two photographs and the cartoon have in common, what are the differences?
   Do you think you can now answer the question:
   "Who is fighting whom in Northern Ireland?"

The conflict seen by a young Protestant from Belfast

"Although the city was then (1961) divided on sectarian lines, it was peaceful. The Protestant McKees lived next door to a Catholic family. 'We used to play with the other side then,' Alcwyn remembers. 'We have bonfires on the 12th July and they helped us collect wood. We helped them for theirs in August. We were just like brothers.'"
The Sunday Times, August 29, 1976

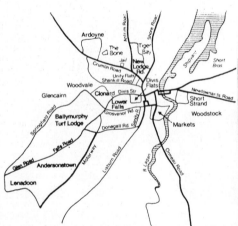

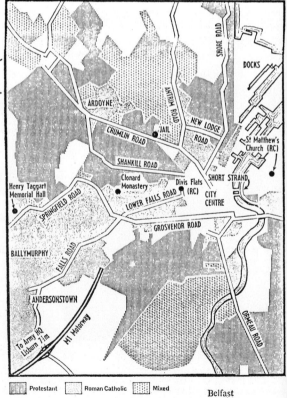

"Belfast, a city divided on sectarian lines"

Belfast, showing Catholic ghettos and hard-line Protestant districts.
Over 70 per cent Catholic in shaded area.
Over 70 per cent Protestant: Donegall Road, Glencairn, Newtownards Road, Sandy Row, Shankill Road, Woodstock Road, Woodvale.

What 7 years of Belfast violence have done to Alcwyn McKee

Chris Ryder talks
to one Belfast teenager
who decribes the bleak
horizons of his life

"We were just like brothers."

ALCWYN McKEE was born in September, 1959, on the Ballymurphy estate on the outskirts of the city. Then a mixed community, it is now totally Catholic and a stronghold of the Provisional IRA. In 1961 the family of four children moved to Brown Square a few hundred yards from Belfast city centre and right on the edge of the staunchly Protestant Shankill Road area.

Although the city was then divided on sectarian lines, it was peaceful. The Protestant McKees lived next door to a Catholic family. "We used to play with the other side then," Alcwyn remembers. "We have bonfires on the 12th July and they helped us collect wood. We helped them for theirs in August. We were just like brothers."

When the troubles began

But in 1969 when Alcwyn was 10 the troubles began; petrol bombs and stones were thrown in his street as the two sides clashed. Alcwyn's first direct experience of violence came one night when the family dog, a fox terrier called Micky, ran off into the Catholic area.

Alcwyn's elder brother Jackie ran after it, calling "Micky, Micky." A group of youths took objection: in Belfast, Micky is not a term much loved by Catholics. The hunt for the dog soon became a full-blown riot, with stones being thrown. Alcwyn takes up the story:

I was sent to my granny's in Sandy Road for safety at first. Then after a few days I was allowed home but I slept in a church hall for a while in case there was any more trouble. Then the army moved in and put up the barbed wire in Coates Street. It was the first time I had ever seen a soldier. I thought their guns were toys. They stayed on the Catholic side of the barbed wire in a straight line across the road. We went down to talk to them. Then one day they came with drills and put stakes in and made the peace line with wire and timber. Some of my friends were throwing stones at the army. The Catholics were throwing at us from behind the soldiers but they turned a big searchlight on us. One of my mates had to throw a stone to break it. I was caught by the tear-gas bombs. I had to get a cold flannel of water on my face. It wasn't funny then.

"We used to have aggro . . ."

In 1971 the McKees moved to a new house in the Lower Shankill area when Brown Square was redeveloped.

There were wire grilles over the window in case of stone-throwing. About the same time I moved to a secondary school in the Crumlin Road. There were Catholic schools nearby and we used to have aggro and punch-ups with them and throw stones. They would come and hit us with belts, but once one of our boys got a Catholic in the eye with a steel comb. The police came to our school for him.

The army mounted "lollipop patrols" every day to try to keep the two sides apart but it didn't work. Then the headmasters of the various schools decided to stagger the home times; we got out an hour before the Catholics.

One day I was chased by two Catholic youths and hit on the forehead with a brick. I went out cold for an hour and was taken to hospital. I got two stitches, two black eyes, and a big swollen nose.

One night they blew up the Criterion Bar across the road. I saw a man shouting, "keep away, keep away". He was stopping cars. Then, bang, there was a big puff of smoke and the bomb went off. The man was blown off his feet and a woman who was crying ran over and said, "You saved my life". He was taken to hospital.

But the worst thing was in 1972 when a close friend was killed. He was a neighbour, Bobby McComb. He was a member of the Ulster Defence Regiment. He took a girl friend home on a Saturday night, and next morning he was found shot through the head, lying on a street corner. He had a hood over his head. The Provisional IRA later claimed responsibility for the murder. I felt rotten. It made me angry. I felt then like doing something about it.

You get good Catholics and bad ones. You can't tell unless they're talking to you. Most Catholics I meet are bad ones who call you names and want to fight but I used to hang about with one and he was all right. Twice I've had stitches, and twice it was the Catholics. The first time in 1969 when I was talking to the soldiers I was hit on the mouth with a brick. I've still got the scar

Out of work

Since he left school a year ago Alcwyn has been out of work. He spends much of his time in the local community centre and never strays far from his home which is surrounded by three Catholic strongholds.

You can't walk down town for clothes even, or you'd get a hiding. If Catholics think I'm a Prod they'll pull me for it. But it works both ways. The Prods pull Catholics too.

It's hard to go looking for a job as well because I'd have to go through Catholic areas. Somebody suggested going to the local technical college to learn a trade but I know a boy was taken from that college and found shot dead in the alley.

I don't think much of the police. They came and saw me once on a suspicion of breaking into cars. They let me out after questioning, but it wasn't fair. I was only passing. They still give us aggro. If you're at the corner, they stop and get out and push you around and ask you what you're doing.

I thought of joining the British army once but I wouldn't now because the soldiers give us aggro too. They call us Irish bastards, and make faces. Anyway, the soldiers always said it's terrible if you join the army.

I won't join the UDA (the Protestant para-military force) either. If you do something wrong, you're liable to be kneecapped. But I do my bit to defend my area. Not too long ago we were up all night in case the Catholics came down to wreck our houses.

" . . . just Paisley . . ."

I don't listen to other politicians, just [Ian] Paisley. But I don't always agree with him. I think he's wrong in condemning the peace movement. I think the bad Catholics have turned on Gerry Fitt now. I heard he got Protestant families houses round here. I would trust [William] Craig but he's too

quiet. Sometimts he loses his head and shouts back for the Protestants but not often enough. Paisley knows what he's really talking about. He never lets anything go.

I don't fancy a united Ireland. That's what the fighting is all about. The Protestants don't want it and the Catholics do. If the SDLP [Fitt's party] don't want a united Ireland, they can be in a power-sharing government. But I don't believe the SDLP. I think they would try to get us into a united Ireland if they get into the government."

From:
Chris Ryder, The Sunday Times,
August 29, 1976

Notes on the text:

a stronghold of the IRA: an area/place where an idea/cause/organisation has a lot of supporters

staunchly Protestant: (of a friend/supporter) firm and loyal

on sectarian lines: (here:) divided into Catholic and Protestant areas

the two sides clashed: had a (violent) confrontation, met in conflict

a group of youths took objection: were against sth., did not like it

became a full-blown riot: (a minor incident) became a violent fight

granny: (coll. for) grandmother

the army moved in: troops were sent to Northern Ireland

barbed wire, stakes, timber: material (wood, pieces of metal, wire etc.) used for setting up barricades in the streets

drill: machine for making holes through hard surfaces/tool

search-light: a movable light (us. big and powerful) used for finding things, people, the enemy (in war).

flannel: a piece of cloth (us. woolen)

wire grille: screen of wire to protect glass, open spaces or similar things

to have aggro: (coll. for) aggression

to give s.o. aggro: to be aggressive to s.o.

punch-ups: (coll. for) fights

to get s.o. in the eye with . . .: to hit s.o. in the eye with . . .

the army mounted "lollipop patrols": the soldiers patrolled streets to look out for (fighting) youngsters

to stagger times: to cause to happen at different times

to go out cold: (coll. for) to faint

he got stitches: the doctor closed his wound with needle and thread

he had a hood over his head: his head and face were covered with a piece of cloth

to claim responsibility for the murder: to say that one/they killed the man

to feel rotten: to feel very miserable

scar: mark/trace left by a cut or wound

local community centre: local meeting place for people of all age groups (us. run by the local council)

to stray far from o.'s home: to go away from/leave o.'s home

to get a hiding: to be beaten

to make faces: make o.'s face look ugly or funny in the small street

you are liable to be kneecapped: you run the (very high) risk of being shot through your knees

I don't fancy a United Ireland: I don't like the idea of a united I.

Glossary:

Ballymurphy estate, Brown Square, Shankill Road, Sandy Road, Lower Shankill area, Crumlin Road: Belfast residential areas on the outskirts of the city, all within the so-called "Belfast Riot Area", where Alcwyn has been living since 1959.

Provisional IRA: "Provisional" wing of the Irish Republican Army (IRA), militant Catholic organisation → *glossary*, p. 117–119

Ulster Defence Regiment: a local part-time military force, established in 1970, its membership is over 97 per cent Protestant → *glossary*

UDA: Ulster Defence Association: hard-line Protestant para-military organisation, formed at the end of 1971. The UDA is heavily armed and has been mainly responsible for the killings of Catholic civilians. → *glossary*

SDLP: Social Democratic and Labour Party → *glossary*

Prod: (coll.) short for Protestant

Ian Paisley, Gerry Fitt, William Craig: three Ulster politicians → *glossary*

12th July/August: important anniversaries for the Protestant/Catholic communities, commemorating historical events

in 1969 . . . the troubles began: after the start of riots in Derry and Belfast 1000 British troops were ordered to Northern Ireland

the army moved in: on the 15th August 1969

Micky: (sl., derog.) Roman Catholic Irishman (from man's Christian name Michael)

peace movement: movement started in August 1976 to end the killing in Northern Ireland, gaining support mainly among women

power sharing: giving a minority (Catholics) a share in governing Northern Ireland

What you have to do

Phrasal Verbs
Structured Vocabulary
Questions on the text
How to interview people

Phrasal Verbs

Learn these words and how they are used:

to put up	– they put up the barbed wire	– to erect, to set up (aufstellen, -richten)
to put in	– they put stakes in	– (einsetzen, hineinstellen)
to blow up	– they blew up the Bar	– to (make) explode, to (make) go into pieces (sprengen)
to blow off	– he was blown off his feet	– to make fall down (by strong air pressure, explosion etc.) (umstoßen, -fegen)
to go off	– the bomb went off	– to be fired, to explode (losgehen)
to turn on s.b.	– the bad Catholics have turned on Gerry Fitt	– to stop supporting s.o. and become hostile to s. o.

Structured Vocabulary – "Semantic fields"

Our text describes the conflict in Northern Ireland through the eyes of a 18-year-old Protestant. It tells us a lot about the scene, the communities involved and the flaring up of the conflict.
Now let us look more closely at what expressions and words are used in the text for describing the two aspects of

Conflict and Communities

We will make two lists of expressions and words referring to these aspects:

List 1: Conflict
These are the words and expressions taken from the 1st part of the text:
Belfast violence
stronghold of the provisional IRA
divided on sectarian lines

Now go on and complete this list for the rest of the text!

List 2: Communities
These are the first few words and expressions referring to "communities":
mixed community
totally Catholic
staunchly Protestant
live next door to

Now go on and complete this list!

Questions on the text

"We were just like brothers"

1. What sort of changes took place in the area where Alcwyn was born?
2. Did the McKee family move away from the city centre in 1961?
3. Did they move to the heart of a Catholic area?
4. Was it dangerous to live in Belfast in the early sixties? (Prove your answer by giving three phrases from the text!)

"When the troubles began"

1. What did the outbreak of violence mean for Alcwyn?
2. When Alcwyn made his first personal experience of violence, was it his brother who had caused the clash by throwing a stone at the other side?
3. How did his parents react after the violent incident had happened?
4. What did the Army do to prevent the two sides from clashing?
5. Did Alcwyn take the soldiers seriously when they moved in?
6. Did he and his friends react in a hostile way towards the soldiers?
7. How did the different groups in the street react towards each other?
8. How did he personally experience that the Army was not playing around with toys?

Questions on the last two passages "Out of work" and ". . . just Paisley . . .":

1. Why is Alcwyn out of work?
2. Does he think that the police are doing a good job?
3. Why has he not joined any military forces so far?
4. What does he think of politicians?
5. Why does he not like the idea of a United Ireland?

How to interview people

Now you take the journalist's part – you ask questions now!

Here are some key words for an interview with Alcwyn McKee on the passage "We used to have aggro . . .":
– going to school
– aggro comes to school
– police
– Army
– headmaster
– personal experience with Catholic youths
– bomb incidents
– worse incidents
– how do you feel about Catholics now?

Who whom? What about?

The immediate causes of the conflict

. . . the picture now being increasingly spread round the world is of a struggle between the British Army and the Catholic community of Ulster, with the Catholic aim being the unification of Ireland. This may be how the conflict now looks, but it is not at all how it began.

The Observer, February 6, 1972

Protestant symbol in Ulster
The red hand of Ulster

According to legend, the captains of two boats – whom some say were Norse chiefs, in search of new territories – sighted the fair land of Ulster on the horizon, and vied with each other to be the first to land and lay claim to it. One, finding his boat just outdistanced by his rival, cut off his hand and flung it to the shore, thereby establishing his claim to possession of the land.

Who is fighting whom?
What is the fight about?

ROBERT STEPHENS and IVAN YATES explain the immediate causes of the Northern Ireland conflict and its escalation.

WHO IS fighting whom in Ulster and what are they fighting about? The questions may sound strange, almost insulting, but as the drama and the horror have increased, so has the confusion. The answers being angrily given now are not always the same as those given by the same people two or three years, or even months, ago.

For example, the picture now being increasingly spread round the world is of a struggle between the British Army and the Catholic community of Ulster, with the Catholic aim being the unification of Ireland. This may be how the conflict now looks, but it is not at all how it began.

Why the British Army moved in

The British Army began to move into Ulster in greater strength and to take over internal security duties as a result of the attacks made by Protestant extremists on Catholic civil rights marchers and on Catholic areas in Londonderry and Belfast in August 1969. The Army's first task was to protect the Catholic areas. It was welcomed by the Catholics as an impartial replacement for the suspect local Ulster (mainly Protestant) security forces.

1967: We shall overcome!

The civil rights movement had been formed in 1967 and held its first demonstration marches—peacefully—in 1968. Its public aims were to reform the social, economic and political structure of Ulster so as to give Catholics equal rights with Protestants inside the province.

Attention was focused on Catholic grievances over local government, public housing, the composition and role of the police and local security forces, and the political system. These included the alleged gerrymandering of constituencies which assured the continued hegemony of the Protestant majority in the main cities.

Part of the background of violence in Ulster is heavy and chronic unemployment. The province has 45,000 out of work in a population of 1,500,000. This is 8.7 per cent of the insured population, twice the rate for the UK as a whole. But Londonderry, with a Catholic majority, has 13.2 per cent unemployed compared with 7 per cent in Belfast.

The civil rights movement disclaimed concern with the traditional aims of Irish nationalism, the unification of Northern and Southern Ireland or changes in the border—except perhaps as a remote ideal. It appeared to accept the constitutional position of Ulster as part of the United Kingdom.

The other forces

But this was not the position of the other force which the events of 1969 brought once more into play, the Irish Republican Army. The official IRA policy was to try to unite the Catholic and Protestant workers on classical Marxist class lines. It rejected violence, partly because an earlier attempt at the violent overthrow of the Ulster regime during 1958-63 had failed through lack of popular support.

But in 1969 a breakaway group, the Provisionals, was formed with the double aim of providing armed protection for Catholic areas against Protestant attack and also of destroying the Stormont regime as a step towards the unification of Ireland.

The Provisionals' strategy

The Provisionals' strategy was to use urban guerrilla war to force the British Government to assume 'direct rule' over Ulster in place of the provincial government and Parliament at Stormont (in other words, itself to remove the Stormont regime).

The conflict would then be turned into a direct confrontation with the British Government and Army. This would force the British to withdraw and so open the way to Irish unity. An important part of the tactics was to destroy the confidence of the Catholics in the British Army's impartiality and so to compel them to look to the IRA as their sole protector and champion.

These tactics have, perhaps inevitably, been largely successful. An escalating cycle of violence has been created in which each official counter-measure against IRA shooting and bombing has alienated further the Catholic community as a whole.

The first important turning point in this process was the revival last summer of 'internment,' the arrest and detention of IRA suspects without trial. A second turning-point was last Sunday's deaths in Londonderry.

What the civil rights movement demanded

The military escalation has overtaken and overshadowed the progress of political reform. The original demands of the civil rights movement were for:—

1. One man, one vote in local elections.
2. The removal of gerrymandering boundaries.
3. Laws against discrimination by local government and the provision of machinery to deal with complaints.
4. Allocation of public housing on a points system.
5. Repeal of the Special Powers Act.
6. The disbanding of the ' B '

Specials, an armed volunteer police reserve, regarded by Catholics as a Protestant political instrument.

Political reforms

Of these demands all have been implemented or are in process of being fulfilled, except for the repeal of the Special Powers Act, which provides for internment.

Local government: One man, one vote in local elections was established in November 1969, i.e., plural voting for business premises and additional residences was abolished. By-elections are already operating under this system.

170 **Ombudsman:** Both a Parliamentary Commissioner and a Commissioner for complaints against local councils and other public bodies were set up in 1969.

Housing: A new Housing Executive responsible for all public authority house-building and allocation was established in March 1971 with a third of its 180 members Catholic.

Police: The Act giving effect to the recommendations of the Hunt Committee became law in March 1970. The Royal Ulster Constabulary no longer has a para-military role and is usually unarmed. The Ulster Specials have been disbanded. The British Army is now responsible for security, assisted by 190 the part-time Ulster Defence Regiment, which is not used for crowd control or riot duties.

From: R. Stephens, I. Yates,
The Observer, February 6, 1972

Notes on the text

confusion: state of being disturbed or puzzled

a picture increasingly spread: an impression getting more and more common or accepted

unification: forming one state out of two or more areas; being united

extremist: a person who holds extreme views

civil rights marchers: people demonstrating peacefully for equal rights of all citizens

impartial: fair, unbiased, not favouring any side

replacement: something or someone put in the place of s.th. or s.o. else

suspect: of doubtful character or quality, not to be trusted

to focus on: to concentrate on

Catholic grievances: (causes for) complaints or demands of the Catholics

gerrymandering: cf. definition p. 67

assure the continued hegemony of s.o.: to make sure that s.o. stays in power and keeps the most influential positions

they disclaimed concern with s.th.: they said they did not care about s.th.

the constitutional position: position accepting the status of Ulster as part of the U.K.

it rejected violence: was opposed to, did not accept violence as political means

a violent overthrow: making s.o./s.th. (e.g. a government) fall or fail by force

a breakaway group: a group which has separated/split off from another group

Stormont: parliament of Northern Ireland up to 1972

to use urban Guerilla war: to use Guerilla tactics in cities

assume direct rule: to take over government or direct political control

destroy the confidence in s.th.: cause people to believe no longer in s.th.

the army's impartiality: an army being impartial or fair

their sole protector and champion: the only one who can protect and fight for them

an escalating cycle of violence: violence that increases and gets worse in the course of events

counter-measure against s.th.: means or action taken against s.th.

turning point: critical state or point of development

the provision of machinery to deal with complaints: providing means or instruments for answering complaints

allocation of public housing: providing and distributing houses or flats (owned by the state or local council) among people

on a points system: grading rights/claims according to certain criteria (e.g. age of people, size of family, children etc.)

to repeal an act: to annul, revoke a law

to disband: to dissolve, break up, keep no longer

to implement s.th.: to carry out or fulfil s.th. (a plan, promise etc.)

plural voting: having more than one vote in one election

business premises: place or building where a firm/business office is situated

additional residence: second or extra place of living

by-election: new or additional election when a councillor or MP has died or resigned

a para-military role: rights and duties similar to military forces

part-time: acting/existing only for some periods of time; opposite of full-time or professional

crowd control and riot duties: actions and measures to deal with large crowds during demonstrations or riots

What you have to do

Structured Vocabulary

Complete our structured vocabulary from this text. Look for words and expressions belonging to the semantic fields of COMMUNITIES and CONFLICT and set up a new one: POLITICS, GOVERNMENT.
Put in this new field all the words and expressions denoting:

political organisations,
political institutions,

the process of law-making and governing etc.
Examples: local government
　　　　 hegemony
　　　　 constitutional position
　　　　 to assume direct rule
　　　　 to repeal an act,
　　　　 etc.
　　　　 Go on!

Version

Translate the first two paragraphs of our text ("Who is fighting . . ." and "Why the British Army . . .") into German.

WHO IS fighting whom in Ulster and what are they fighting about? The questions may sound strange, almost insulting, but as the drama and the horror have increased, so has the confusion. The answers being angrily given now are not always the same as those given by the same people two or three years, or even months, ago.
10 For example the picture now being increasingly spread round the world is of a struggle between the British Army and the Catholic community of Ulster, with the Catholic aim being the unification of 15 Ireland. This may be how the conflict now looks, but it is not at all how it began.

Why the British Army moved in

The British Army began to move into Ulster in greater strength and to take over internal security duties as a result of the attacks made by Protestant extremists on Catholic civil rights marchers and on Catholic areas in Londonderry and Belfast in August 1969. The Army's first task was to protect the Catholic areas. It was welcomed by the Catholics 10 as an impartial replacement for the suspect local Ulster (mainly Protestant) security forces.

Prepare statements for short speeches in class!

Look up the information given in the text and use the drawings as visual aids!

(Teamwork)

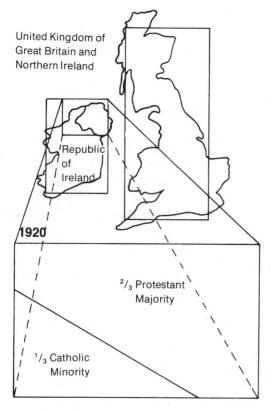

United Kingdom of Great Britain and Northern Ireland

Republic of Ireland

1920

²/₃ Protestant Majority

¹/₃ Catholic Minority

Northern Ireland = Ulster
half-autonomous "province" of Britain up to 30 February 1972, when "direct rule" was introduced

Team 1

"The province of Ulster up to the 1960s"

Prepare an introductory statement explaining the following points:
– the constitutional position of Ulster
– the two communities
– the continued hegemony of one of the communities
– the political aims of the other one

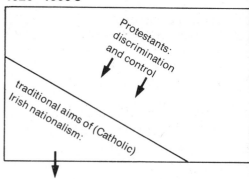

1920–1960 s

Protestants: discrimination and control

traditional aims of (Catholic) Irish nationalism:

1 unification of Northern and Southern Ireland
or
2 changes in the border

Team 2

"The civil rights movement"

Prepare a statement on the civil rights movement in Ulster explaining the following points:
– 1967
– the movement's public demands and aims
– its political strategy
– its success or failure

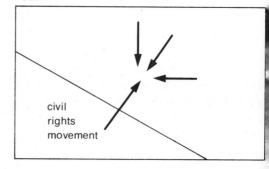

1967

civil rights movement

Team 3

"The British Army in Ulster"

Prepare a statement on the changing role of the British Army in Ulster. Explain the following points:
– 13. 8. 1969
– the reactions of the two communities to the British Army in 1969
– Compare the journalists' report and Alcwyn McKee's view on this event
– the changing role of the British Army as a consequence of the Provisionals' strategy
(Comment shortly on the journalists' view that "these tactics have, perhaps inevitably, been largely successful!)

13. 8. 1969

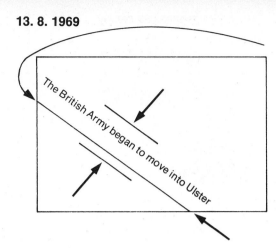

Team 4

"The IRA"

Prepare a statement on the IRA explaining the following points:
– the IRA as "the other force" in Ulster up to December 1969 (cf. the glossary)
– the two IRAs ("the split")
– the strategy of the Provisional IRA
– What does the term "direct rule" mean?
– What do the two journalists imply by stating "These tactics have, perhaps inevitably, been largely successful

1969

Introducing a long story in Ireland

PUTTING THE CLOCK BACK

What
you have
to do

Analysing a cartoon

Have a first glance at the cartoon – what hits your eye?

Is it
- the writing on the wall
- the man with his outfit
- the shopping bag – or rather its contents?

all

1. Have a closer look now at the person. What is he doing? *He is putting a time-bomb into his bag.*
Do you think he is repairing his clock? *No, surely not!*
When you try to find out what the man is doing – is the caption of any help to you? *Yes, the man is from the IRA. The IRA tries to unite the Catholics and Protestant +*
May be we cannot take the caption in its literal sense. What does it tell you?

2. Try and say what is going on in the cartoon. *The man prepares his bag for a fight*
Where is the man going to place the time bomb?
What is he aiming at? Who/what is he going to blow up?
If you look at the caption again: do you think the cartoonist uses this caption in its literal sense? *yes, he wanted to show from where he comes.*
Does it tell you anything about the cartoonist's view of what the man is doing?
What does the cartoonist express by using that phrase figuratively?

The phrase has two meanings:
1. putting back the time
2. remember 1690 (Battle against the catholic supporters)

3. What about the writing on the wall? *
Can you see any relation between the caption and the slogan on the wall?
Before you can tell what 1690 means you have to get further information!
You can look up the passage on William of Orange and the Battle of the Boyne further on in this book (p. 36).*
This date is very important for the Protestants in Ulster ("the major feast in the Protestant calendar") and is solemnly commemorated every year!
You know: the person in the cartoon is a member of the Irish Republican Army, i.e. he is an Irish Catholic.
How will he remember that date 1690?

+ workers on classical Marxist class lines.
⚹ the writing on the wall should remember the Battle of the Boyne of 1690
the IRA stands of the side of the catholics. Every year the IRA remember the Battle which the catholics had lost

The author wanted to show his point of view)

* William III of Orange fought the Battle of the Boyne in 1690 against the Catholic supporters of his father-in-law, the Catholic King James II, and defeated them decisively. William supported the English "Glorious Revolution" which caused James to leave England and look for support in France and Ireland.

4. What is the cartoonist's message?
   Make up your mind:
   He encourages the IRA to go on.
   He reminds the English public, the average reader of the historical background of the conflict in Ulster.
   He warns the Irish communities not to fight the old battles again.
   Take all aspects of the cartoon into consideration!

Written Analysis

To sum up our discussion of the cartoon:
Write a short analysis, summing up our description in about 150 words.

1171

17 76
~~17 98~~

POBLACHT
THE PROVISI
IRISH
TO THE PEOP

1920

Part 2:
A long story in Ireland
800 years of
Anglo-Irish history

1171

The first English conquest of Ireland (1171)

Henry's legacy was at least twofold: His being there marked the very beginnings of the so-called settlements and therewith an increasingly feudal, colonial relationship between England and Ireland.

(Ronald Hindmarsh, Lecture on "The Irish Question" given in Dillingen, 14. 10. 74)

Henry II the man who had Archbishop Becket murdered, was the first English ruler to take troops to Ireland; and the potential enemy he had in mind, in 1171, was his own Norman barons. He wanted to make sure that they did not use Ireland to establish rival principalities in. The sheer size of his army was enough to win a titular lordship of Ireland for the English crown.

(J. Whale, The Sunday Times, Jan. 13, 1974)

In the event a large number of baronages and earldoms were created for the officers Henry had left behind as settlers.

In order to do that he drove out a good many Irish aristocrats. This is the beginning of the settlements of English and Scottish people in Ireland.

This was to the great resentment of the Irish, who suddenly found themselves being evicted from their estates by the alien English and often employed by them as servants and menials.

Henry's legacy was at least twofold: His being there marked the very beginnings of the so-called settlements and therewith an increasingly feudal, colonial relationship between England and Ireland.

In due time this gave rise to the interesting theory that, in fact, Ireland is the first part of the British Empire and a sort of testing ground on which the English evolved the techniques that they could much later apply on a world-wide scale, particularly in the 19th century.

The increasing tension between the foreign settlers and the local natives, who objected to their robber-baron methods, very soon erupted into violence. This racio-religious conflict very soon settled into a pattern of behaviour which has been the same ever since, namely, in the first instance, suppression of the natives by the settlers as a reaction to this, terrorism against the settlers by the natives and, as a reaction to that, counter-terrorism on the part of the settlers against the natives.

This is the pattern of violence which repeated itself all the way down in Irish history from the 1170s to the 1970s virtually without intermission.

(R. Hindmarsh, loc. cit.)

Notes on the text:

to establish rival principalities: the setting up or founding of (small) countries or areas which are ruled by princes and/or barons and threaten royal power

titular lordship: having the title of a Lord of Ireland without exercising power.

Henry's legacy: the effects of his policy, having long-lasting consequences.

to evolve techniques: to develop and practice means and methods

racio-religious conflict: a conflict having two important aspects: one of race (Gaelic-English), the other of religion (between the old Irish Catholic religion with many pagan elements and orthodox Roman Catholicism of the English settlers. This is different from the 16th cent. when the English came to Ireland as Protestants!)

virtually without intermission: (a conflict of 800 years) without any major interruption or pause.

What you have to do

Questions on the text
Guided comment

Questions on the text

What relationship was established by Henry II?

What conflict arose out of that relationship?

What pattern evolved out of that conflict?

Guided comment

"World and Press" published a long article "Background to the troubles" as "A short history of Ireland in two parts" in August/September 1976. The author of this historical background analysis, Carol M. Claxton, begins her article with the following paragraphs. Read these paragraphs carefully and write a short comment on them, using the following questions as a guide line (80–100 w.).

IRELAND has been an inhabited, civilised *bewohnt* and troubled country for a long time. The first inhabitants were the Picts, followed by Celtic immigrants during the 4th century BC. Druidism probably originated in Ireland. By about AD 350–400 Christianity began to be a power in the country. From Ireland Christian missionaries spread all over Europe to carry the Gospel. This strong religious streak has stayed with the Irish to the present day.

At the turn of the 8th century the Norsemen began to undertake plundering raids on the coast and even far inland. There followed a long period of serious unrest, *Unruhe* with frequent changes of kings, until the early 12th century. Less than a hundred years later, the Anglo-Normans invaded the country and established enclaves, despite opposition by the native Irish. The ups and downs continued, *fortsetzen* with intermarriages, *Mischehen* rebellions, and the attempt to consolidate English rule.

(Carol M. Claxton, Background to the Troubles. A short history of Ireland in two parts. In: "World and Press", August/September 1976)

1. C. M. Claxton does not mention *erwähnen* King Henry II, the first English ruler to take troops to Ireland. Explain why Henry II's conquest *Eroberung* of Ireland is important for understanding the Anglo-Irish conflict.

2. What is the difference between dating a short history of Ireland back to the 4th century and dating it back to 1171?

basis
to conquer
to invade

invasion
to occupy
occupation army

to get divorced
essential
crucial

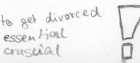

33

1541
1649
1690

British settlement in Ireland

If you re-read Anglo-Irish History by the light of recent events, one fact leaps to eye. For eight centuries England's view of Ireland was a coldly strategic one. The English were in Ireland to bolt England's back door against sea-borne foreign enemies – France, the Netherlands, and especially Spain. Their aim was to keep Ireland from falling to the enemies of the English state – enemies sometimes inside England, but mostly outside. It was not until the middle 1960s that the nature of war had changed enough to make that preoccupation look as old-fashioned as it was unprincipled.

(John Whale, "The End of a Long Story in Ireland", Sunday Times, January 13, 1974)

The Tudor Conquest
16th—17th Century

Henry VIII, reasserting English influence after more than three centuries during which its area had shrunk to a Pale round Dublin, got himself proclaimed (in 1541) king of Ireland. "The Tudor monarchy," writes Professor J. C. Beckett, "could not for ever tolerate the existence of
10 a half-subdued dependency which, if not controlled by England, might soon be controlled by England's continental enemies."

Mary, Henry's elder daughter, continued his policy through the first (and unsuccessful) plantations of English colonists.

Elizabeth I, her half-sister,
20 fought a nine-year war against Hugh O'Neill – The O'Neill, a great Ulster noble – during which he had the help of a Spanish fleet. James I was on the throne before the Irish commanders lost the war and (in 1607) left the country: he put English and Scottish settlers on their land to secure Ireland a-
30 gainst Spain in particular, and

several hundred were well established before he was engaged in a new Spanish war.

(J. Whale, loc. cit.)

Elizabeth I. 1603. Completed the Tudor conquest of Ireland begun by her father, Henry VIII (in a tradition established by Henry II). The chief aim was to bolt England's back door against sea-borne foreign enemies – France, the Netherlands, and especially Spain

James I. 1607. Put English and Scottish settlers in Ulster as a garrison: Spain was still an intermittent enemy of England

The Cromwellian Settlement

Cromwell. 1649. Went to Ireland after Charles I's execution to root out Royalist rebels against the Commonwealth

Cromwell, the Englishman best remembered in Ireland, went there in 1649 partly on an anti-Catholic crusade: the island had been little touched by the Reformation. But his chief mo-tive was to deny beaten Royalists a mustering-point. Charles I had just been executed: a week before that, the future Charles II had been invited to Ireland to gather together his considerable support there. It may have been because Cromwell lost his temper, as Lady Antonia Fraser suggests in her new book about him, that he allowed his troops to kill between 2,000 and 4,000 people in Drogheda. But Drogheda was a Royalist-held fortress which commanded the approaches to the troublesome North; and to make a prize and an example of the town at the outset of the campaign made brutal strategic sense.

Cromwell's method of holding territory thus subdued was to clear out all those landlords who were not provenly pro-Commonwealth ("Let them go to hell – or to Connaught," he is supposed to have said) and to replace them with new ones. Many of these settlers had been officers in the Commonwealth armies: all were Protestants.

From then on, Protestants of English and Scottish origin were a permanent force in Ireland. They made up the bulk of the landowning and ruling class; and it was successive administrations in London which had put them there, out of straightforward military self-interest. As guarantors of safety to the regime in England, they had a special title to its protection in return. The essential difference between Catholic and Protestant was therefore not one of doctrine (though in the atmosphere of the early seventeenth century that could not be unimportant, and it has kept some importance to this day): it was the difference between native dispossessed and alien possessors.

(J. Whale, loc. cit.)

Notes on the text:

Henry VIII. (Tudor): King of England 1507–47
reassert: re-establish, make effective again
shrunk: (Past of **shrink**) become smaller
Pale: area round Dublin, controlled by the English
Mary ("Bloody M."): Catholic Queen 1553–58
noble: baron, aristocrat, landlord of high rank
to be engaged in s.th.: to take part in, work at, be busy with
garrison: military place where troops are stationed
intermittent: coming and going, stopping and starting again
Oliver Cromwell: *1599–1658*
Leader of the radical "Independent" (Puritanist, Calvinist) opposition against the crown. Had Charles I (1625–49) dethroned and executed. Abolished monarchy. Was supported by (mainly) Protestant gentry and citizens.

crusade: "Kreuzzug"
mustering point: a place where soldiers are gathered and/or engaged
Drogheda: strategic place on the east coast (near the river Boyne), conquered by Cromwell 1649
troublesome: causing trouble, difficulties etc.
to make a prize: to conquer and plunder (a town)
to subdue: to conquer, overcome
to clear out: to throw out, to remove
proven: clear, reliable, obviously true
the bulk of s.th.: the majority of s.th.
successive: following (one after the other), next
straightforward: direct
guarantor: s.o. who gives security or a guarantee for s.th.

The Battle of the Boyne

William III. 1690.
Defeated James II, who was using French help in ·Ireland to try to recover the English throne he had lost

William of Orange confirmed the Protestant supremacy when he defeated his Catholic father-in-law James II at the Battle of the Boyne, near Drogheda, in 1690 and he has his picture on gable-ends in the Protestant slums of Belfast still, to prove it. That campaign also neatly demonstrated the hostile purposes to which Ireland might be put if it were not thus garrisoned. James, with the help of Louis XIV. of France, was seeking to use Ireland as a base for the recovery of the crown which he had already lost to William in England. The Boyne put paid to the attempt. *(J. Whale, loc. cit.)*

By the end of the century almost all the land of Ireland was in the hands of new owners, and the old land owning class, the Old English and native Irish gentry and aristocracy, were dispossessed.

In Ulster, all Protestants, all the colonists, felt that they had earned and shared in a victory, which they saw as one for freedom, religion and laws over royal absolutism, popish superstition and Gaelic barbarism.

In the . . . country . . . a colonial class of English origin and Protestant religion, landowners and townsmen, found themselves in a position where they could exploit freely the great mass of the people, defeated, alien in religion and culture, leaderless. They proceeded to do so.

(de Paor, Divided Ulster, p. 16–17)

Notes on the text:

ascendancy: domination, hegemony, control
to confirm: to make firmer and stronger
supremacy: dominance, control
on gable-ends: on the upper part of the front wall of houses
neatly: clearly, distinctly
hostile purpose: aims, intentions of the enemy
to put s. th. to a purpose: to use for a specific p. or aim

to garrison (a town or country): to station troops in a (military) place
the recovery of the crown: getting back the crown, become king again
to put paid to s. th.: to put an end to s. th.
superstition: unreasonable or false belief in s. th. supernatural, magic etc.
exploit: use for o.'s own personal advantage or profit, make unfair use of s. o.
alien: foreign, unfamiliar

The British settlement in Ireland

1171:	Henry II.
16th/17th cent.:	the Tudor conquest of Ireland
1649:	the Cromwellian settlement
1690:	William of Orange/ the Battle of the Boyne

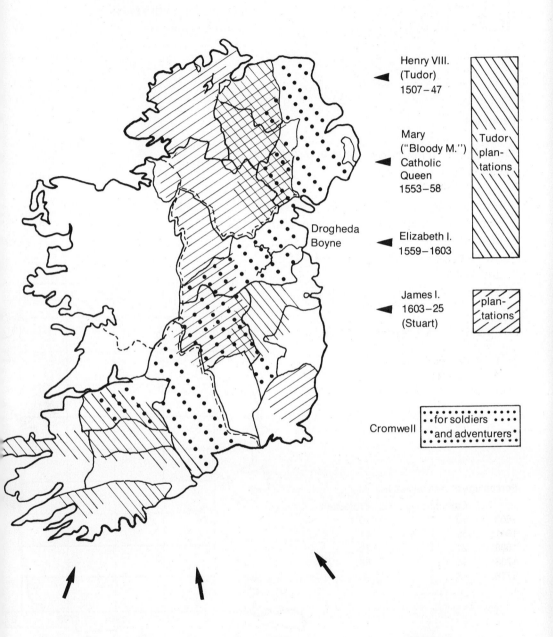

Henry VIII.
(Tudor)
1507–47

Mary
("Bloody M.")
Catholic
Queen
1553–58

Tudor
plan-
tations

Drogheda
Boyne

Elizabeth I.
1559–1603

James I.
1603–25
(Stuart)

plan-
tations

Cromwell

• for soldiers • •
• • and adventurers •

England's foreign enemies:
Spain, France, Netherlands

Map from:
Ruth Dudley Edwards,
An Atlas of Irish history,
London 1973, p. 159 ff.

What you have to do

Diagram fill-in
Questions on the texts
Guided summary

Diagram

The transfer of land ownership in Ireland
1603–1778

1. Have a look at the figures first.
2. Put in the figures in the graph and draw the lines of the transfer of land ownership in Ireland between 1603 and 1778.

Percentage of land owned by

	Catholics	Protestants
1603:	90	10
1641:	59	41
1688:	21	79
1703:	14	86
1778:	5	95

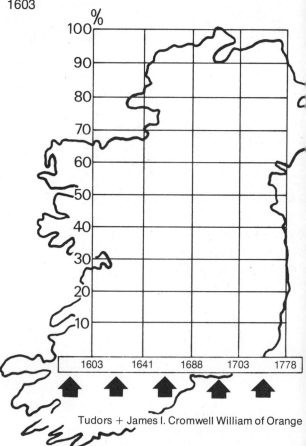

Tudors + James I. Cromwell William of Orange

38

Questions on the Texts

1. Tudor Conquest

   What had happened to the English influence up to the 16th century in Ireland?

   How did Henry VIII reassert British influence in Ireland?

   What alternatives did Henry VIII have – according to a history professor's view?

   How did the kings and queens of England secure their influence in Ireland?

2. Cromwell

   Did Cromwell change the policy of his royal predecessors?

   Why is Cromwell the Englishman best remembered in Ireland?

   What antagonism arose after Cromwell's rule?

3. William III of Orange

   What events and symbols are today associated with William of Orange?

   What was it that the Protestants thought they had fought for or against?

   What was the result for the Protestant classes in the long run?

Summary

The making of a colony

Summarize shortly the process of colonization in Ireland by relating the figures of the diagram above to the historical facts.

Concentrate on the following points:
Conquest (Henry II)
Plantations and settlements (Tudors)
Rooting out of opponents (Cromwell)
Final dispossession of the old landowning class (William of Orange)

The United Irishmen's Insurrection

The United Irishmen

Founded in 1791 in Belfast, the United Irishmen was a revolutionary democratic society spurred on by the example of the AMERICAN COLONISTS, influenced by the FRENCH REVOLUTION and dedicated to establishing an independent democratic Republic in Ireland.

Its founders were Wolfe Tone, a Dublin Protestant, and a group of middle-class Presbyterians in Belfast.

It had considerable support among Northern Presbyterian weavers, then the most radical group in Ireland, and aimed to unite them with the discontented masses of the Catholic population. The United Irishmen were in direct contact with France and hoped to stage a rising with French support. The rising took place in 1798 in Antrim and Down in the North and Wexford in the South but was easily defeated. A French Expedition arrived two months too late, in August 1798, and was defeated as well.

(M. Farrell, Northern Ireland: The Orange State, p. 364–365)

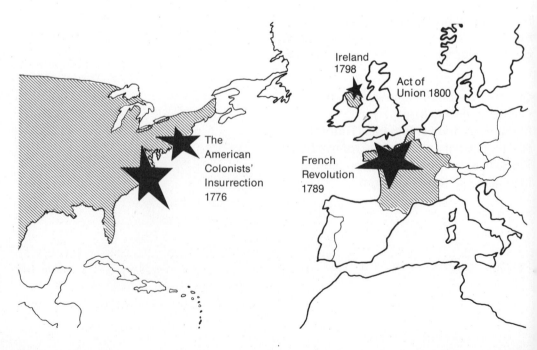

Ireland 1798

Act of Union 1800

The American Colonists' Insurrection 1776

French Revolution 1789

France was the enemy which stimulated the next major change in Ireland. By the 1800 Act of Union the whole country was absorbed into the United Kingdom and the subordinate Irish parliament abolished. A brief rebellion in 1798, against the disabilities which Irish Catholics suffered under penal legislation, had been inspired by the French Revolution; and now that the Revolution had turned militarily expansionist Ireland could not be left unsecured.

Britain and France were at war: a Franco-Spanish fleet was stationed off Brest

(J. Whale, loc. cit.)

Pitt the Younger. 1800. Brought a rebellious Ireland formally under the British Parliament to secure it during a French naval war

Notes on the text:

Presbyterians: Protestant group, very strong among settlers of Scottish origin, stressing the equality among their members including ministers (dt. Calvinisten)

to stage a rising: to start a rebellion

to suffer disabilities under penal legislation: being discriminated against by laws, e.g. Irish Catholics were not allowed to hold land as personal property

What you have to do

Answer the following questions:

1. Did the leader of the United Irishmen come from the Catholic masses?
2. Where did the rebellion get support from?
3. Compare the course of events in America and Ireland at the end of the 18th century!
4. What were the results of the rebellion for Ireland?

Extra material

Ireland 1798 – America 1776

Ireland 1798

Spurred on by the example of the American colonists ... and influenced ... by the French Revolution. The United Irishmen developed as a revolutionary movement demanding an independent democratic Republic with full equality for the Catholic majority of the population.

(Farrell, p. 13)

Settlers and Natives

Not only Roman Catholics suffered disabilities in eighteenth-century Ireland. Dissenters also – and there were Quakers, Huguenots, and others as well as Presbyterians – were discriminated against although in much smaller measure than the Catholics (especially after 1719). They had made common cause with the established church against King James, and would continue to do so against Stuart pretenders, but they were not part of the ascendancy or the establishment, and they were given no more toleration or acknowledgement of their rights and needs than was deemed expedient. English policy in mercantile and industrial matters operated against them to the advantage of English products. At the same time, for most of the eighteenth century, they had little inclination to make common cause with the oppressed Catholics. Very large numbers of Ulster Presbyterians indeed escaped from their dilemma in the eighteenth century by migrating to America as their forefathers had migrated to Ireland from Scotland, seeking the democratic freedoms which dissenters in general so often sought in the seventeenth and eighteenth centuries, and which so often they were reluctant to extend to others. Ulster Presbyterians, or 'Scotch Irish', played their part later in the century in establishing, in the name of freedom, the United States, a slave-owning republic like those of antiquity.

This migration to some extent counteracted the effect of the inward flow of migration from Scotland in the seventeenth century. The Scots-Presbyterian bridgehead east of the Bann was not extended westward at full strength, and much of Ulster remained Gaelic-speaking through the eighteenth century. Indeed, on a local scale, Irish poetry and culture even flourished at times, especially in the south-east of the province, and in Antrim itself there were many Irish speakers. The mixture of English-language and Irish-language cultures, the development of the 'Ulster custom' in land tenure, the spread and development of the tradition of home crafts, all combined to give Ulster a more distinctive character than it had possessed in its now distant Gaelic past, while at the same time the plantation and settlement culture had over the years and decades gradually adapted itself to its environment. The northern Presbyterians were no longer Scots, but 'Scotch-Irish', Ulstermen – a distinctive kind of Irishmen, but still increasingly conscious of being Irishmen, with interests distinct from those of the English.

In the later eighteenth century the population of Ireland was increasing rapidly, and with this rise pressure increased on the land. In Ulster the pressure accentuated the division on the one hand between Protestant landlords and Protestant tenants and on the other between Protestant and Catholic tenants. *(de Paor, p. 19–20)*

British restrictions on Irish trade in the 18th century

By the end of the eighteenth century ... some of the descendants of the settlers were beginning to chafe under control from London. A thriving commercial and industrial class was developing in Ireland, especially in the North where the better terms on which the settlers held their land enabled them to accumulate some capital, and where the linen industry was taking root. But government restrictions designed to protect industry in Britain hindered the growth of industry in Ireland. *(Farrell, p. 13)*

The war in America gave the colony the opportunity to assert itself. When France and Spain entered the war in support of the American colonists, the English government found itself without available troops to defend Ireland against invasion, and the Protestant ascendancy throughout the country met the emergency by forming volunteer corps. Having armed to defend the government's policy, they found themselves in a position to emulate the Americans and take effective action on their own grievances. At a great volunteer parade in Dublin in 1778 a cannon was displayed with a placard reading 'Free trade or this', and after the British surrender in America a convention of the Ulster volunteer corps at Dungannon demanded legislative independence for the colonists in Ireland. The Whig government which replaced Lord North's made concessions: the Dublin parliament was freed from the control of the Westminster parliament, Irish trade was freed from some of the restrictions which had hampered it. But while legislative independence was thus achieved by the colony, the London government in effect retained full control over the Irish executive. And 'divide and rule' remained the instinct of the executive in Dublin Castle, an instinct which had long been successfully acted on in Practice.   *(de Paor, p. 20–21)*

The United Irishmen

But efforts to reform the parliament failed and, influenced now by the French Revolution, The United Irishmen developed as a revolutionary movement demanding an independent democratic Republic with full equality for the Catholic majority of the population.

The United Irishmen found their greatest support in the growing commercial town of Belfast, among the prosperous tenant farmers of North Down and South and Mid-Antrim, and among Presbyterians who resented the privileges of the Anglican church – the church of the landlords and the aristocracy. But the United Irishmen never had the support of the majority of Ulster Protestants. Antagonism between Catholic and Protestant was still strong in many areas and was reinforced by competition for land tenancies. After a series of skirmishes in Armagh and Tyrone the Orange Order* was formed in 1795 as a militant Protestant organisation dedicated to preserving Protestant supremacy, and it immediately began driving Catholics out of parts of North Armagh and South Tyrone . . .
                        (Farrell, p. 13–14)

The crushing of the rebellion in 1798

The crushing of the rebellion (in 1798) snuffed out the spirit of republicanism, but for some years the allegiance of Northern Protestants was divided between Orangeism and liberalism, with liberalism still strong among Belfast businessmen and Orangeism entrenched among the landlords and the most backward tenant farmers.

The British government had responded to the '98 Rebellion with The Act of Union (1800), abolishing the Dublin parliament and integrating Ireland with the United Kingdom.
                        (Farrell, p. 14)

The effects of the rising

The effects of the risings of 1798 and their bloody suppression were deep and lasting. Pitt decided to deal with the urgent problem of Ireland by forcing through a union of the two kingdoms of Ireland and England with a single parliament in Westminster. On the Irish people, north and south, the rising made a deep impression. It marks the beginning of modern Irish nationalism in the full sense, for it made the first break between the Gaelic past and the era of participation in political mass movements of one kind and another for the Catholic masses of the people. For the Protestant people of Ulster it marks a turning point too: the radical republicanism, the levelling egalitarianism, which seemed natural to the self-reliant Presbyterian spirit and for which Belfast especially was noted in the late eighteenth century, had led the merchants and tradesmen and small farmers of Antrim and Down to open their minds to the ideas of liberty, equality, and, most remarkable of all, fraternity, and to contemplate joining with their Catholic fellows in making another America in Ireland. That spirit was distracted by the remarkable and rapid growth of Orangeism from 1795 (initially largely among Anglicans in the areas where there were large numbers of Catholics); it was cowed and crushed by the brutal pacification of northeast Ulster carried out by General Lake before the risings and by the ruthless suppression of the rebellion; it was dismayed by the stories of vengeance exacted on Protestants in the Wexford rising. The year of terror and misery an-

---

* Orange Order = "Politico-religious organisation dedicated to maintaining Protestant supremacy and the link with Britain. No Catholic and no-one whose close relatives are Catholics may be a member. Founded in Co. Armagh in 1795 during Catholic-Protestant clashes over land, it spread quickly, with some government encouragement, throughout Ulster and among Protestants in the rest of Ireland. The Orange Order declined in importance during the nineteenth century but revived in the 1880s when Home Rule became a serious possibility, and many prominent and respectable Unionists joined it. With its banners, sashes and parades and its fiercely anti-Catholic rhetoric it has been very effective in mobilising the Protestant masses in the Unionist cause. It has also frequently been the instrument of discrimination and patronage. The Orange Order is still strongly represented in the official Unionist Party and the UUUC."
                        (Farrell, p. 357–358)

swered, among others, the question whether the Protestant lower orders in Ulster would combine with the Catholics against landlords and rulers, or would combine with landlords and rulers against Catholics. The Dublin administration divided Ulster and ruled it.   *(de Paor, p. 32)*

Ulster, especially Belfast prospered

The restrictions on industry and trade were lifted and Ulster, especially Belfast, prospered under the Union. Steam power revolutionised the linen industry, an engineering industry developed and eventually shipbuilding as well. The population of Belfast jumped from 20,000 in 1801 to 100,000 in 1851 and 350,000 in 1901. Belfast was becoming a major industrial city like Birmingham or Glasgow. Its industries depended on Britain for their markets and towards the end of the century they began to share in the benefits of the expanding Empire. The Belfast businessmen and merchants quickly forgot their former nationalism and republicanism and became strong supporters of the Union – after all they now had a vested interest in it.

(Farrell, p. 14)

America 1776
The final chapter of American colonial history was also written abroad, for the restrictive policies of British mercantilism provided an economic impetus to the American Revolution, just as the natural rights philosophy of the European Enlightenment set its ideologiacal framework.   *(Heffner, p. 10)*

The roots of American society

Freed from the tyrannical economic, political, and ecclesiastical restraints of the Old World, and blessed with a bountiful environment whose rich and abundant resources, varied climate, and vast domain imbued in him an unquestioned faith in his own future, the American was in truth a "new man." Yet the roots of American society were firmly implanted in the great traditions of Western civilization, and ultimately American nationality was as heavily indebted to its European heritage of ideas and mode of life as it was to the new environment. Indeed, in its inception and its development, American colonial history was clearly a reflection of European experiences. The discovery of America resulted from the breakup of the feudal system, the rise of the nationstate, the revival of commerce, and the search for trade routes to the fabulous riches of the East. Later, the long process of English colonization of the New World was motivated both by the quest for free religious expression stemming largely from the Protestant Reformation of the sixteenth century, and by that desire for economic opportunity which had its origins in the middle-class business ethic peculiar to the modern Western world.

The final chapter of American colonial history was also written abroad, for the restrictive policies of British mercantilism provided an economic impetus to the American Revolution, just as the natural rights philosophy of the European Enlightenment set its ideological framework. Mercantilism, an economic arm of the rising nationalism of the seventeenth and eighteenth centuries, had as its major objectives national self-sufficiency and prosperity for the dominant merchant and banking class. A favorable balance of trade was particularly important to the mercantilist doctrine, for if more goods and services were sold abroad than were imported, gold and silver would come into the country and the nation's total economic strength would be augmented rather than depleted. Each nation desired a favorable balance of trade, however, and so the great mercantilist powers of Europe soon turned to overseas possessions as a source of economic strength. For these colonies existed solely to be exploited by the mother country – to produce essential raw materials cheaply, to provide an unlimited market for surplus manufactured goods, and to offer a minimum of economic competition.

British colonial policy

British colonial policy amply demonstrated the mother country's intention of molding her American possessions into this mercantilist pattern. To free herself from dependence upon foreign nations for needed raw materials, the Navigation Acts of the seventeenth and eighteenth centuries listed various "enumerated commodities" (such as sugar, tobacco, indigo, and naval stores) which the colonials had to export to England alone. And in an effort to retain exclusive control of the rapidly growing American markets for British manufactured goods, all foreign commodities bound for the colonies were required to pass through England, where prohibitive export duties and freight and handling charges made transshipment intolerably expensive. Competition by the industrious colonists themselves was nearly eliminated through laws such as the Woolens Act (1699), the Hat Act (1732), and the Iron Act (1750), which prohibited or discouraged local efforts at manufacturing.

Though mercantilism benefited the colonists in certain respects – generous bounties, for instance, were paid for indigo and badly needed naval stores, and a monopoly of the English tobacco market was insured to the American producer – the economic well-being of the colonies was for the most part harshly subordinated to the needs of the mother country. Even the Southern settlements, whose staple crops – such as tobacco – well suited them for the colonial role, were hard pressed by the one-sided mercantilist system.

The eve of the American Revolution

And by the eve of the American Revolution Thomas Jefferson estimated that a persistently unfavorable colonial balance of trade had placed at least half of the tobacco planters of Maryland and Virginia hopelessly in debt to British creditors. At the same time the various Navigation and Trade Acts attempted to restrict severely the trading, shipping, manufacturing, and other economic activities of the settlements in the North, where climate and soil were not capable of supporting the large scale cultivation of staple crops for the home market. Yet the colonies prospered, at least in the New England and Middle Atlantic regions. Smuggling and other evasions of mercantilist measures were prevalent, and for long decades before the conclusion of the French and Indian War in 1763, the British were too thoroughly immersed in a bitter imperial rivalry with France to enforce their restrictive legislation.

With the defeat of France, however, the British were able to bring to an end the era of "salutary neglect" and to turn their full attention once again to strict enforcement of colonial policy. Besides, Parliament now strongly reasserted its right to legislate for colonials who had long known virtual independence and self-rule and who were well versed in the liberal philosophy of the eighteenth-century Enlightenment. Political discontent was thus added to economic dislocation, and economic grievances soon found expression in the loftiest principles of political liberty. Royal (and even Parliamentary) efforts to enforce mercantilist policies were damned as contrary not only to the rights of Englishmen, but to the "natural rights of man" as well, while the colonists' fundamental antipathy to taxation of any kind achieved immortality in the idealistic slogan "no taxation without representation." The British were unmoved by these protests and in rapid succession the Sugar Act (1764), the Currency Act (1764), the Stamp Act (1765), the Townshend Duties (1767), the Tea Act (1773), and the Intolerable Acts (1774) taxed and regulated the colonial economy and imposed the severest restrictions upon colonial self-government.

A growing sentiment for independence and separation from the mother country

The colonists were quick to reply. A Stamp Act Congress met in October, 1765, to denounce the hated tax on newspapers, magazines, commercial papers, and other documents, and an organization of patriots known as the Sons of Liberty directly forced the resignation of nearly all of the imperial stamp agents. American merchants agreed not to import British merchandise until the tax was repealed, and many persons stoutly refused to buy any stamps at all. Even though colonial pressures finally effected the repeal of the Stamp Tax, the tide of unrest continued to rise. Americans more and more frequently joined together to oppose imperial measures; and after British soldiers had fired into a jeering Boston mob (the "Boston Massacre" of march, 1770) popular resentment increased tremendously. Non-importation agreements, "Committees of Correspondence" (which Samuel Adams of Massachusetts organized to inform patriots throughout the colonies of current affairs), the "Boston Tea Party" of December, 1773, and finally the First Continental Congress that met in Philadelphia in September, 1774 – all of these actions marked a growing sentiment for independence and separation from the mother country. And though there were many who still opposed the final break with England, the Revolution began in earnest in April, 1775, at Lexington and at Concord bridge, where "embattled farmers stood and fired the shot heard round the world."

Declaration of Independence
4 July 1776

Tom Paine's enormously popular and influential pamphlet, "Common Sense," published anonymously in January, 1776, quickly helped solidify Americans' rebellious spirit. And in June, 1776, a resolution that "these United Colonies are, and of right ought to be, free and independent states" was offered before the Second Continental Congress by Richard Henry Lee of Virginia. Then on July 4 the Congress formally adopted (with modifications) Thomas

190 Jefferson's draft of the Declaration of Independence. The Declaration expressed certain fundamental precepts: that all men are equally endowed with the self-evident natural rights of life, liberty, and the pursuit of happiness, that civil government is merely an instrument to guarantee these rights within the framework of social order, that when government becomes tyrannical the social compact is broken and it is the "right of the people to alter or to abolish it." These were 200 precepts which clearly embodied the political tenets of the European Enlightenment. Thus for Americans whose intellectual heritage was largely European, and whose free environment as well was conducive to libertarian ideas, the Declaration (as Jefferson himself later wrote) expressed not "new ideas altogether," but rather the "common sense of the matter ... the harmonizing sentiment of the day." Pre-eminently it was an eloquent "expression of the American mind," 210 and to those who cherished the democratic faith of their fathers it was to remain for all times the fountainhead of American ideology.

(Heffner, p. 9—12)

What you have to do

Guided Analysis
Summary
Comment

Guided Analysis

Answer the following questions:

1. Both Ireland and America were British colonies in the 18th century. In what way can the colonists in America be compared with the colonists in Ireland, in what way were they different? What about the natives in both countries?
2. Was the long process of British colonisation in America motivated in the same way as the one in Ireland?
3. Did Britain's colonial policy in America run along the same economic and political lines as in Ireland?
4. Mercantilism is said to be "an economic arm of the rising nationalism" of the 17th and 18th centuries in America. Is that equally true for Ireland?
Why was American nationalism different from Irish nationalism at that time?

5. Was the imperial rivalry with France more dangerous to Britain in America than in Ireland?
6. Why did Britain finally manage to continue dividing and ruling in Ireland, why did Britain fail in America?
7. Do you agree with the following statement:
"Had we (= Britain) won that fight (= in America at the end of the 18th century) ... we would have had something far worse than Ireland on our hands. And bigger. We would have had, for a long time, a large dependency bleeding by our side, embittered, frustrated, neurotic and inevitably moving an uncontainable explosion that would have left us snarling antagonists – perhaps for ever ..."

(The Observer, July 4, 1976)

Summary

Write a summary (about 150 words) using the answers to the questions above as a basis. Your summary should give an answer to the following question:

"Why didn't Ireland – unlike America – manage to become an independent democratic republic at the end of the 18th century?"

Comment

1. Text

After the deposing of James II in England because of his Catholicism, the Irish supported him, and in 1689 he landed in the country from France and raised an army. He was defeated at the Battle of the Boyne in 1690 and returned to France, leaving the Irish to ruin themselves in his cause. Their heroic stand at Limerick was the last fight of Catholic Ireland as a nation in arms.

From this time on, Englishmen and Protestants were given legal prefence; Catholics were barred from carrying arms, teaching publicly, and practising the law. But by the 18th century the Irish Protestants began to resent their political and economic subjection to English interests. A political party appeared among them, inspired among others by Jonathan Swift, and by the end of the century the claim of the people of Ireland to be bound only by their own laws and courts had been admitted by England. The events of the American Revolution also played a role in putting Ireland for the first time in Irish hands – though those hands were those of the Protestant ascendancy. However, Catholic oppression was also eased, and Catholics were allowed to purchase lands freely and have their own schools.

(C. M. Claxton, Background to the "Troubles", A short history of Ireland in two parts (Part I) World and Press, 2nd August Issue, 1976)

2. Questions

Does Mrs. Claxton give a correct historical account of events in Ireland at the end of the 18th century?

Comment on the following answer a student wrote to this question:

"Mrs Claxton is right in some details, but she leaves out several others. The United Irishmen were a liberal group and their members were not confined to the Protestant community. They were inspired by the spirit of democracy of the age and were influenced not only by the American Revolution but by the French Revolution in 1789, too. When she speaks of less oppression on the Catholics, she forgets that this was confined only to the Catholic upper-class, whose members were not as militant as the mass of the people. It is not true that their claims were admitted by England. Why then the "Act of Union" which brought about direct rule?

The Great Famine (1840s)

The potato famine explains a lot. It began in 1845. In that year, the population of Ireland was eight million. In 1858, the population had diminished to four million. One and a half million had died. The rest had cleared out. The word "genocide" has been used, but it is too strong a term. What happened in the Irish potato famine was not the deliberate destruction of a race; it was caused by the inability of a system founded on colonial conceptions of state assistance to adjust itself to catastrophe. A lesson should have been learned. It wasn't. One of the people who emigrated in 1847 was a John Kennedy of Wexford, whose great grandson became President of the United States.

(Irish Liberation, An Anthology, ed. Ulick O'Connor, p. 11)

A famine funeral, 1847

By the Act of Union passed in 1800, Ireland joined Scotland and Wales as part of the United Kingdom, ruled by one Parliament in London. The Scots and the Welsh managed to live fairly happily and peacefully under the Union; the Irish did not. Why was this . . .?

The root of the problem was that Ireland was a mainly Roman Catholic country ruled by Protestant foreigners, colonial administrators acting on behalf of a Protestant Government far away . . .

To add to the hardships of the Irish, most of their land was owned by English Protestants, foreigners who spent most of their time away from their estates and who would not, or could not afford to, spend the capital to improve them. The poor tenants were left to the mercy of the landlords' agents, who demanded ever higher rents. The peasant was liable to be deprived of his miserable possessions very often a mud hut on a tiny plot of wretched land — at a moment's notice. These smallholdings were constantly divided up into even smaller units to provide for the ever increasing population, which at the beginning of the 19th century was growing faster than in any other country.

(Jackdaw, No 61, I)

Rents were spent in England or on the Continent; in 1842 it was estimated that £ 6,000,000 of rents were being remitted out of Ireland

(C. Woodham-Smith, The Great Hunger, p. 16)

The peasants lived on potatoes, and when the potato crop was killed by disease, famine struck. In the Great Famine of 1845–9, about one million people died (about one-eight of the total population) and another million emigrated, mainly to America. Ireland is the only country in modern times to suffer a continued drop in population. By 1951 her population was scarcely more than half its 1841 figure. *(Jackdaw, No 61, I)*

In 1841 the population of Ireland was given as 8, 175, 124; in 1851, after the famine, it had dropped to 6, 552, 385, and the Census Commissioners calculated that, at the normal rate of increase, the total should have been 9,018, 799, so that a loss of at least $2^1/_2$ million persons had taken place"

(C. Woodham-Smith, loc. cit. p. 409)

The English were blamed for the disaster of the famine. Some criticism was unfair, but starving people do not take a reasoned and balanced view. The hungry Irish could not understand why their crops of wheat should be sent to England while they were left to die. They could not understand why the English Government — always so willing to pass laws to damage Irish trade and economic interests — should refuse to give more help; they put it down, like everything else, to English wickedness.

(Jackdaw, No 61, I)

Figures were produced in the House of Commons giving the amounts of grain and cereals exported from Ireland to England for a period of, roughly, three months from the date when the potato failure was established up to February 5, 1846. 258,000 quarters of wheat and 701.000 hundredweight of barley, worth about a million pounds, had left Ireland with, in addition, 1.000.000 quarters of oats and oatmeal; and since February 5 export had been continuing at the same rate.

(C. Woodham-Smith, loc. cit. p. 70)

Ireland was helpless: almost wholly an agricultural country, she did not have the natural resources to develop into a modern industrial state, and she was tied by the Act of Union to a strong neighbour who was rapidly becoming industrialized. To England her own economic interests came first and Ireland's a long way last.

(Jackdaw, No 61, I)

In the four provinces of Ireland the smallest loss of population was in Leinster, 15.5%, then Ulster, 16%, Connaught's loss was greatest, 28.6%, and Munster lost 23.5%. In some respects, death and clearance improved Ireland; between 1841 and 1851, nearly 360,000 mud huts disappeared, the greatest decrease being 81 per cent. in Ulster, which then included the distressed county of Donegal, followed by Connaught, with a decrease of 74 per cent., Munster 69 per cent., and Leinster 62 per cent... Between 1848 and 1864... thirteen million pounds was sent home by emigrants in America to bring relatives out, and it is part of the famine tragedy that, because no adequate measures of reconstruction were undertaken, a steady drain of the best and most enterprising left Ireland, to enrich other countries.

(C. Woodham-Smith, loc. cit. p. 409–410)

Union was a failure in both countries. In Ireland it produced administration which was remote and (especially at the time of the famine in the 1840s) cruel: in England it clogged government by bringing able and obstructive Irish parliamentarians to Westminster. The Liberals under Gladstone ("My mission is to pacify Ireland", he said in 1868) proposed Irish home rule: the Conservatives fought it by fair means and foul for half a century, confident in their own imperial mission and making full use of the strategic argument. *(Sunday Times, January 13, 1974)*

liable to be deprived of: the peasant had to reckon that his belongings were taken away
at a moment's notice: without any warning
smallholding: small area of land given to a tenant farmer
Census Commissioners: people dealing with the official counting of a population

to clog government by the presence of able and obstructive parliamentarians: to stop government business by parliamentary means like long speeches
by fair means and foul: they used all possible techniques, just and unjust

What you have to do

Guided Analysis
Summary

Guided Analysis

Answer the following questions:
1. Is it true that the potato was the only food plant grown on a large scale in Ireland?
2. Is it true that the famine stopped the agricultural exports completely?
3. Why did the standard of living of the farms continue to decrease? (Give two reasons!)
4. What was typical of the relationship between English landlords and Irish tenants?
5. What were the results of the famine for Ireland? (at least two effects!)
6. Why was Union a failure, according to the text?
7. What did Liberal policy/Conservative policy aim at in Ireland in the 19th century?

Summary

"The Great Famine in Ireland"
Write a summary of about 150 words, referring particularly to the causes of such a disaster and the consequences for the whole of Ireland.

Extra material

Brendan Kennelly

My Dark Fathers

My dark fathers lived the intolerable day
Committed always to the night of wrong,
Stiffened at the hearthstone, the woman lay,
Perished feet nailed to her man's breastbone.
Grim houses beckoned in the swelling gloom
Of Munster fields where the Atlantic night
Fettered the child within the pit of doom,
And everywhere a going down of light.

And yet upon the sandy Kerry shore
The woman once had danced at ebbing tide.
Because she loved flute music – and still more
Because a lady wondered at the pride
Of one so humble. That was long before
The green plant withered by an evil chance;
When winds of hunger howled at every door
She heard the music dwindle and forgot the dance.

Such mercy as the wolf received was hers
Whose dance became a rhythm in a grave,
Achieved beneath the thorny savage furze
That yellowed fiercely in a mountain cave.
Immune to pity, she, whose crime was love,
Crouched, shivered, searched the threatening sky,
Discovered ready signs, compelled to move
Her to her innocent appalling cry.

Skeletoned in darkness, my dark fathers lay
Unknown, and could not understand
The giant grief that trampled night and day,
The awful absence moping through the land
Upon the headland, the encroaching sea
Left sand that hardened after tides of Spring,
No dancing feet distrubed its symmetry
And those who loved good music ceased to sing.

Since every moment of the clock
Accumulates to form a final name,
Since I am come of Kerry clay and rock,
I celebrate the darkness and the shame
That could compel a man to turn his face
Against the wall, withdrawn from light so strong
And undeceiving, spancelled in a place
Of unapplauding hands and broken song.

From the book Selected Poems by Brendan Kennelly.
© Allen Figgis & Co. Ltd., Dublin, and Brendan Kennelly
1969. Brendan Kennelly (1936–). Born in Ballylongford,
County Kerry. Associate Professor of English at Trinity
College, Dublin.

Brendan Kennelly, a young Irish poet, has written
of what the famine meant to his generation almost
one hundred years after. The following is his
introduction to his poem "My Dark Fathers."

5 In "My Dark Fathers" I tried to define my
own relationship with Irish history. One day I
attended a talk given by Frank O'Connor about
the famine that happened in Ireland in the nineteenth century and had such harrowing effects on
10 the Irish character. I was trying, at the time, to
write a poem about that history, which I had lived with since childhood. During his talk,
O'Connor spoke of a traveler's (Mrs. Asenoth
Nicholson) description of a woman dancing on
15 the Kerry shore:

This woman, who danced before me, was more
than fifty, and I do not believe that the daughter of

illustration: Brad Holland

Herodias herself was more graceful in her movements, more beautiful in her complexion or sym-
20 *metry, than was this dark-haired matron of the mountains of Kerry.*

This image struck me immediately. The woman was the entire people, capable of spontaneous artistic expression; capable of it, that is,
25 before the famine. But then came the terrible desolation. O'Connor made me aware of Peadar O Laoghaire's *Mo Sgeal Fein,* where there is the following description of the dead and dying:

You saw them there every morning after the
30 *night out, stretched in rows, some moving and some very still, with no stir from them. Later people came and lifted those who no longer moved and heaved them into carts and carried them up to a place near Carrigastyra, where a big deep pit*
35 *was open for them, and thrust them into the pit.*

This is "the pit of doom" in my poem. There is a description of a man named Paddy bringing his wife Kate from the workhouse back to his hut:

Next day a neighbor came to the hut. He saw
40 *the two of them dead and his wife's feet clasped in Paddy's bosom as though he were trying to warm*

them. It would seem that he felt the death agony come on Kate and her legs grow cold, so he put them inside his own shirt to take the chill from
45 *them.*

In the poem I identify this woman, dead from famine disease, her "perished feet nailed to her man's breastbone", with the woman comparable to the daughter of Herodias, dancing on the
50 shore of Kerry. Perhaps the most frightening consequence of famine is described in George Petrie's collection *The Ancient Music of Ireland:* the terrible, unbearable silence. To my mind, this meant not only the silence that followed racial
55 suffering akin to what Hitler inflicted on the Jews, but it meant that Ireland became the grave of song. I was witnessing the death of the dance:

This awful, unwonted silence which, during the famine and subsequent years, almost everywhere
60 *prevailed, struck more fearfully upon their imaginations, as many Irish gentlemen informed me, and gave them a deeper feeling of the desolation with which the country had been visited than any other circumstance which had forced itself*
65 *upon their attention.*

(*Irish Liberation, loc. cit., p. 11–15*)

What you have to do

Understanding the poem

Answer the following questions

1. What is the general mood of the poem "My dark fathers"?
2. Which lines/phrases/words reflect the mood most adequately?
3. How can you tell that the poem is about Ireland and an event in Irish history?
4. Paraphrase the lines "... That was long before – The green plant withered by an evil chance;"!

5. What might the dancing woman stand for?
6. How is the people's character affected by the disaster?
7. In what way are the introductory notes given by the author helpful to you?
8. Which lines of the poem are related to the picture?

POBLACHT
THE PROVISI
IRISH
TO THE PEOP

The Easter Rising (1916)

We declare the right of the people of Ireland to the ownership of Ireland, and to the unfettered control of Irish destinies, to be sovereign and indefeasible. The long usurpation of that right by a foreign people and government has not extinguished the right, nor can it ever be extinguished except by the destruction of the Irish people.

(The Easter Proclamation, 1916)

The Rising was crushed after a week of fierce fighting and the leaders shot; but it changed the mood of the nationalist population. They would no longer be satisfied with limited Home Rule within the British Empire. They wanted an independent Republic, they had no more faith in British parliaments and they were prepared to support the use of force to get what they wanted. The stage was set for confrontation.

(Farrell, p. 20)

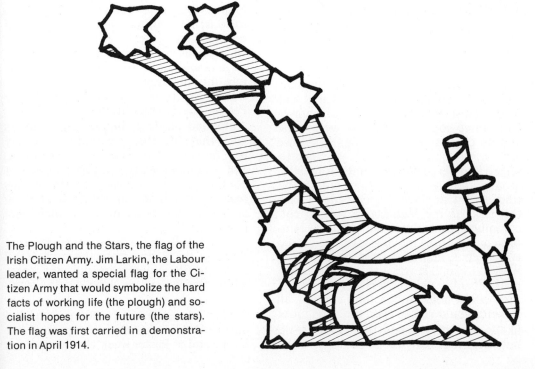

The Plough and the Stars, the flag of the Irish Citizen Army. Jim Larkin, the Labour leader, wanted a special flag for the Citizen Army that would symbolize the hard facts of working life (the plough) and socialist hopes for the future (the stars). The flag was first carried in a demonstration in April 1914.

The Rising

On Easter Monday, April 24th, 1916, the fierce nationalism of the Irish patriots erupted in an armed uprising, known ever since as the "Easter Rising".

The Rising was the work of a small body of men, organized and led by a tiny group. The forces at their command were unbelievably small: the Irish Citizen Army, only a few hundred men, all in Dublin; and the Irish Volunteers. In 1916 the Volunteers numbered about 16,000 men, the majority in the provinces. Only one in five had a service rifle. Those in country districts had shotguns, but many had no weapons at all. They had no machine-guns and no artillery.

The Volunteers were not only a small force but a divided one as well. Their Chief of Staff, Eoin MacNeill, opposed any armed insurrection. Unlike many Volunteers, MacNeill was not a member of the I.R.B., the body that really organized the Rising. The plans were laid by the Military Council of the I.R.B., the seven men who signed the Proclamation of Independence. They kept their plans from MacNeill and, if he disapproved, they were determined to "go it alone".

It is hard now to tell what their plans were; all seven leaders were executed and took their secrets with them to the grave. Only three copies of the plan were made and no original is known to exist. All we can say is that the rebels planned to seize a number of strong-points in Dublin, around the city's centre and within the ring of British garrisons. Outside Dublin the task of the Volunteers was to cut communications, prevent British reinforcements from moving into the capital and keep a line of retreat open to the West of Ireland. It was a strictly defensive plan. Possibly the leaders hoped that if they could hold Dublin long enough, all Ireland would rise to their aid. It is more likely that they knew they would fail, but believed that their courage, their blood sacrifice, would be an example that would one day set all Ireland ablaze.

Plans were made to enlist German aid, but they all went wrong. Sir Roger Casement went to recruit an Irish Brigade from prisoners of war in Germany, but failed. Disappointed and disillusioned, almost ready to call off the Rising, Casement returned to Ireland by submarine. On Good Friday he stepped ashore and was arrested almost immediately. In America, the I.R.B. arranged for a German ship, the Aud, to land 20,000 rifles and ammunition in support of the Rising. Owing to a muddle over dates, the Aud found no one waiting to meet her. Discovered by a British ship, the German captain was forced to scuttle his craft.

Worse was to follow. The plans for the Rising could not be revealed to MacNeill; he had to be tricked. A routine mobilization was announced for Easter Sunday. In reality this was the signal for the Rising. MacNeill found out and was furious; he countermanded the order at once. When he heard of the Aud plan he changed his mind; when it failed he changed his mind again. His final order, cancelling mobilization, was published in the Dublin papers on Easter Sunday morning. Pearse, the military leader of the Rising, pretended to agree, but secretly told his men that the Rising would start a day late, on Easter Monday. So over the weekend Volunteer leaders received a series of conflicting orders. Not all the orders reached everybody and not all of them arrived in the order in which they were issued.

The result was a total confusion that doomed the Rising from the start. Many rank-and-file Volunteers did not know whom to believe or what to do; many stayed at home. In the provinces, only 2,000 of the expected 10,000 men turned out. In Dublin, 5,000 were expected, but by the end of Easter week the rebels there

Tom Clarke, the veteran Irish Republican Brotherhood leader, was one of the most revered men in the Irish freedom movement. Despite his age – he was 58 – he fought in the G.P.O. and was executed on May 3rd, 1916.

Padraig Pearse, As Director of Organization of the Irish Volunteers and a member of both the Supreme Council and the Military Council of the I.R.B., Pearse was a key man in the Rising. As a link between these two bodies, he was perhaps the natural choice as military Commander-in-Chief. An inspired teacher and a fine poet, Pearse was the "soul" of the Rising. He was executed on May 3rd, 1916.

numbered no more than 1,600. The rebels had not enough men to seize the most important positions in Dublin, such as Dublin Castle or the Shelbourne Hotel, and they made the big mistake of choosing the G.P.O. as headquarters instead of the Bank of Ireland or Trinity College. The G.P.O., hemmed in by other buildings, had no real military value — it was merely a good place from which to fly the flag of the new Republic. Although Trinity College was held only by a few soldiers on leave, with some undergraduates and members of the O.T.C., the rebels left it alone, and British reinforcements were able to use its commanding position to fire on large areas of the city.

These and other mistakes, such as the failure to seize the Telephone Exchange, can probably be put down to inexperience. The Volunteers were part-time soldiers who had never been in action. They found that a civil war is hard to fight; you have to fight in your own home town, in front of friends, wives, sweethearts. This needs courage of a peculiar kind. Courage the Volunteers had; and decency too. They were pathetically anxious to do the right thing — one group hurrying to their posts commandeered a tram, but insisted on buying tickets, fifty-seven tuppennies! There was no drunkenness or looting. Their good example was not followed by civilians: scores of drunken men and women from the slums broke into jewellery and drapers' shops, decking themselves out in rings and fine clothes; children stormed the toy- and sweet-shops. Neither the looters nor their more prosperous fellow citizens cared anything for the rebels' cause. On Bank Holiday Monday, Dubliners returned from a fine day at the seaside or the Irish Grand National to find roads blocked and railway lines shut, to hear shooting in the streets. Rumours flew — the Germans had landed, the British fleet had been destroyed, there were a hundred German submarines in St Stephen's Green pond! Dubliners were confused and angry, some actively hostile, pouring abuse on men fighting for their lives. The rebels had no chance. The British brought in reinforcements, threw cordons round the main Irish positions and drew the net tight. Only as the end came did Dublin's hostility begin to change to sympathy; although they did not know it, the rebels had begun to win the fight for Irish freedom.

(From: Jackdaw No 61)

The rising itself lasted a week. The whole tragic farce . . . was nevertheless enough to re-emphasise luridly the dangers of a disloyal Ireland.

The effect was two-fold. Caught at a nervous stage of the war against Germany, the Asquith Government felt obliged to have 15 of the Dublin insurgents shot. They were picked out unsystematically over several days; and their martyrdom turned the IRB into an army, a national movement capable of sustaining a fight against the British forces of order (chiefly the irregular Black-and-Tans) for two-and-a-half years after the war was over. By contrast, the loyal Protestants in the North looked even more precious than before; and the British Government grew prepared to see Ireland divided rather than lose them altogether.

(J. Whale, loc. cit.)

The years from 1918 to 1923 were to be dramatic ones throughout Ireland. They were to see the ousting of the old Home Rule Party (United Irish League = UIL) by Sinn Fein, the establishment of an illegal Irish parliament in Dublin in defiance of Westminster, and the outbreak of a War of Independence against British rule in Ireland (1919–1921).

In the North the violent confrontation between Unionist and Nationalist which had been looming for so long was finally to erupt. The outcome would be partial independence for the bulk of the country in the new Irish Free State, and partition leaving the six north-eastern counties under British rule in the United Kingdom – but with local self-government.

(Farrell, p. 20–21)

Notes on the text:

I. R. B.: Irish Republican Brotherhood = a revolutionary secret society dedicated to establishing an Irish Republic by force. It was first known as The Fenians and organised an unsuccessful rising in 1867 and a bombing campaign in England. It was reorganised as the IRB in 1873 and eventually infiltrated the Sinn Fein party and the Irish Volunteers. It was the IRB which planned the 1916 Rising and reorganised the Volunteers into the IRA in 1918–19.

to set Ireland ablaze: to set on fire e.g. by bombs

to enlist German aid: to win German support

to scuttle his craft: to sink o.'s own ship

to doom The Rising from the start: condemn to failure

rank-and-file Volunteers: ordinary soldiers

G. P. O.: General Post Office (in Dublin)

O. T. C.: Officers' Training Corps

pathetically anxious: anxious in a way that excites pity

looting: take away goods unlawfully

luridly: in a shocking way, violently

Black-and-Tans: Special forces recruited in England on a semi-mercenary basis to reinforce the Royal Irish Constabulary during the War of Independence. The Black and Tans were recruited largely from unemployed ex-service men and wore khaki uniforms with black police caps and belts-hence the name. They were brutal and undisciplined. They served in Ireland from 1920 to 1922 and at the peak period there were 7,000 Black and Tans in the country.

to oust: to force sb. out . . . and take over their position

to loom: to appear in vague, threatening shape

What you have to do

Guided Analysis
Comment

Guided Analysis

Answer the following questions:

1. Was the Easter Rising 1916 a rebellion with broad popular support?
2. What sort of people organized the Rising?
3. Do you think that the rebels stood a good chance against the British at any stage of the rebellion?
4. What were the plans of the rebels?
5. Were the leaders of the Rising confident about the outcome?
6. What role did Germany play in the Easter Rising?
7. Does John Whale in The Sunday Times, January 13, 1974, take a different view of Germany's role?
8. What does the author mean with "these and other mistakes"?
10. How did the Dubliners react towards the Rising?
11. Why did the British Government crush the rebellion relentlessly?
12. In what way did the failure of this rebellion turn out to be the beginning of a successful fight for Irish Independence?
13. Is there any link between the Easter Rising 1916 and the Partition of Ireland in 1920?
14. Do you think the rebels were right to rise in arms in 1916?
15. Do you agree with the following statement: "The Easter Rising is another example of the Irish discrepancy between inefficiency and bravery?"

"For eight centuries England's view of Ireland was a coldly strategic one. The English were in Ireland to keep it from falling to the enemies of the English state – enemies sometimes inside England but mostly outside . . .
Germany, this time, proved this point.
During the First World War the Irish Republican Brotherhood, flag-carriers of nationalism, maintained that the cause of Irish liberty would be best served by a German victory; and the Germans were just sufficiently interested, at the time of the Dublin rising of Easter 1916, to send a small shipload of arms and a submarine carrying Roger Casement and a rubber dinghy. The arms vessel, intercepted by the Royal Navy, blew itself up in Cobh harbour. Casement (Ulsterman, former British consular official and the IRB's envoy in Germany) fell out of the dinghy and stumbled ashore to be picked up by two Irish policemen."

Comment

Write a short comment (about 200 words). Use the answers to the questions above as a basis of your comment:

"The Easter Rising 1916—another one of the Irish rebellions that failed *or* the beginning of a successful fight for Irish independence?"

Extra material

Introductory Note

2,500 copies of the Proclamation were printed in the basement of Liberty Hall on Easter Sunday morning, April 23rd, 1916, for distribution the next day. The machine on which they were printed was old and dilapidated; and there was such a shortage of large type (the kind used for newspaper headlines) that the Proclamation had to be printed in two operations. The type could not be inked properly, so there were many smudges in most surviving copies. Each copy was signed by the printer and compositor as proof that it was genuine.

Padraig Pearse – who read out the Proclamation from the General Post Office to a small, rather indifferent Bank Holiday crowd on Easter Monday – and James Connolly probably wrote most of it, but it is likely that all seven signatories had a hand in it. It is signed "on Behalf of the Provisional Government"; the signatories were the members of the Military Council of the Irish Republican Brotherhood, which had planned the Rising. In fact, the constitution of the I.R.B. laid down that the President of the Irish Republic, if and when it was formed, was to be the current President of the Supreme Council of the I.R.B. This was Denis McCullough, who should have been President of Ireland if the Rising had succeeded. During Easter 1916, however, he was in Belfast, and took no part in the Rising.

(Jackdaw, No. 61, Notes 4)

What you have to do

Questions on the text

Questions on the text

1. If you compare the Proclamation of the Irish Republic 1916 with the American Declaration of Independence is it justified to speak of a "discrepancy between rhetorical pretensions and reality" as far as the Proclamation is concerned?

2. In what way were the political aims of the United Irishmen similar to the aims of the Irish Republican Brotherhood, in what way were they different?

3. The Proclamation of the Irish Republic states the aims for which the rebels were fighting.
   Which of these aims have been achieved by now?

POBLACHT NA H EIREANN.

THE PROVISIONAL GOVERNMENT
OF THE
IRISH REPUBLIC
TO THE PEOPLE OF IRELAND.

IRISHMEN AND IRISHWOMEN: In the name of God and of the dead generations from which she receives her old tradition of nationhood, Ireland, through us, summons her children to her flag and strikes for her freedom.

Having organised and trained her manhood through her secret revolutionary organisation, the Irish Republican Brotherhood, and through her open military organisations, the Irish Volunteers and the Irish Citizen Army, having patiently perfected her discipline, having resolutely waited for the right moment to reveal itself, she now seizes that moment, and, supported by her exiled children in America and by gallant allies in Europe, but relying in the first on her own strength, she strikes in full confidence of victory.

We declare the right of the people of Ireland to the ownership of Ireland, and to the unfettered control of Irish destinies, to be sovereign and indefeasible. The long usurpation of that right by a foreign people and government has not extinguished the right, nor can it ever be extinguished except by the destruction of the Irish people. In every generation the Irish people have asserted their right to national freedom and sovereignty; six times during the past three hundred years they have asserted it in arms. Standing on that fundamental right and again asserting it in arms in the face of the world, we hereby proclaim the Irish Republic as a Sovereign Independent State, and we pledge our lives and the lives of our comrades-in-arms to the cause of its freedom, of its welfare, and of its exaltation among the nations.

The Irish Republic is entitled to, and hereby claims, the allegiance of every Irishman and Irishwoman. The Republic guarantees religious and civil liberty, equal rights and equal opportunities to all its citizens, and declares its resolve to pursue the happiness and prosperity of the whole nation and of all its parts, cherishing all the children of the nation equally, and oblivious of the differences carefully fostered by an alien government, which have divided a minority from the majority in the past.

Until our arms have brought the opportune moment for the establishment of a permanent National Government, representative of the whole people of Ireland and elected by the suffrages of all her men and women, the Provisional Government, hereby constituted, will administer the civil and military affairs of the Republic in trust for the people.

We place the cause of the Irish Republic under the protection of the Most High God, Whose blessing we invoke upon our arms, and we pray that no one who serves that cause will dishonour it by cowardice, inhumanity, or rapine. In this supreme hour the Irish nation must, by its valour and discipline and by the readiness of its children to sacrifice themselves for the common good, prove itself worthy of the august destiny to which it is called.

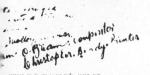

Signed on Behalf of the Provisional Government,

THOMAS J. CLARKE,

SEAN Mac DIARMADA,   **THOMAS MacDONAGH,**

P. H. PEARSE,   **EAMONN CEANNT,**

JAMES CONNOLLY.   **JOSEPH PLUNKETT.**

DUBLIN No. OF THE EASTER RISING, DUBLIN 1916.   PRINTED IN GREAT BRITAIN.

Extra material

William Butler Yeats (1865–1939)
Easter 1916

W. B. Yeats, who won the Nobel Prize for Literature in 1924, is regarded by many as the greatest poet of the twentieth century. Yeats involved himself deeply in the political affairs of the Ireland of his time.

He was a 'public man' from early in his career. As a very young man he joined the Irish Republican Brotherhood, the secret physical force organization which plotted the 1916 rebellion. In 1922 he became a senator of the new Free State, and took an active part in its deliberations.

(Irish Liberation, p. 17)

Yeats is Ireland's greatest poet, not least because he learned to confront the challenging complexities of Irish life. He recognized that Ireland is always capable of treachery and squalor, but he was also aware of its capacity for heroism and nobility. He witnessed and experienced 'the weasel's twist, the weasel's tooth'. Yet he exhorted later generations to be, and to continue to be, the 'indomitable Irishry'.

(The Penguin Book of Irish Verse, Introduction, p. 40)

Yeats had known many of the leaders of the 1916 rebellion, some of whom, poets and writers, had worked with him on magazines or in the theater. After the rebellion, he realized, with the instinct of the poet, that an event had taken place which could change the course of history. Written within a year of the rebellion, Easter 1916 shows Yeats' remarkable insight into the national mind at that time. *(Irish Liberation, p. 21)*

Easter 1916

I have met them at close of day
Coming with vivid faces
From counter or desk among grey
Eighteenth-century houses.
5 I have passed with a nod of the head
Or polite meaningless words,
Or have lingered awhile and said
Polite meaningless words,
And thought before I had done
10 Of a mocking tale or a gibe
To please a companion
Around the fire at the club,
Being certain that they and I
But lived where motley is worn:
15 All changed, changed utterly:
A terrible beauty is born.

That woman's[1] days were spent
In ignorant good-will,
Her nights in argument
20 Until her voice grew shrill.
What voice more sweet than hers
When, young and beautiful,
She rode to harriers?
This Man[2] had kept a school
25 And rode our winged horse;

This other[3] his helper and friend
Was coming into his force;
He might have won fame in the end,
So sensitive his nature seemed,
30 So daring and sweet his thought.

This other man[4] I had dreamed
A drunken, vainglorious lout.
He had done most bitter wrong
To some who are near my heart,
35 Yet I number him in the song;
He, too, has resigned his part
In the casual comedy;
He, too, has been changed in his turn,
Transformed utterly:
40 A terrible beauty is born.

Hearts with one purpose alone　　*The stone's in the midst of all.*　　*To know they dreamed and are*
Through summer and winter seem　*Too long a sacrifice*　　　　*dead; And what if excess of love*
Enchanted to a stone　　　　　*Can make a stone of the heart.*　*Bewildered them till they died?*
To trouble the living stream.　　*O when may it suffice?*　　　　*I write it out in a verse —*
The horse that comes from the road, 60　*That is Heaven's part, our part* 75 *MacDonagh and MacBride*
The rider, the birds that range　　*To murmur name upon name*　　*And Connolly and Pearse*
From cloud to tumbling cloud,　　*As a mother names her child*　　*Now and in time to be,*
Minute by minute they change;　　*When sleep at last has come*　　*Wherever green is worn,*
A shadow of cloud on the stream　*On limbs that had run wild.*　　*Are changed, changed utterly:*
Changes minute by minute;　　 65 *What is it but nightfall?*　　 80 *A terrible beauty is born.*
A horse-hoof slides on the brim,　*No, no, not night but death;*
And a horse splashes within it;　　*Was it needless death after all?*
The long-legged moor-hens dive,　*For England may keep faith*
And hens to moor-cocks call;　　*For all that is done and said.*
Minute by minute they live:　　 70 *We know their dream; enough*

[1] This was Constance Gore-Boothe, a beautiful young Anglo-Irish aristocrat who fought in the rebellion in 1916 and was condemned to death, but afterward reprieved. She was the first woman M.P. elected to the British Parliament in 1919. She died in 1927.

[2] Patrick Pearse, commandant-in-chief of the Insurrectionary Forces in 1916. Executed after the Rising.

[3] Thomas MacDonagh, professor of literature, University College, Dublin, one of the six signatories of the 1916 Proclamation and commandant of the Insurrectionary Forces at Jacob's Factory. Also executed after the Rising.

[4] This is Major John MacBride, who married Yeats's beloved Maude Gonne. MacBride had fought in the Boer War against the British, and, hearing there was a battle taking place in Dublin at Easter, hurried to the city to take part in it. His only request when he was executed was that his captors not bind his eyes. "I have been looking down rifles all my life," he said.

What you have to do

Understanding the poem

Understanding the poem

Answer the following questions:

1. What structures the poem in the first place?
2. a) How many parts can you discern?
   b) Sum up the different parts by giving them headings!
3. How is the poem related to Easter in the Roman Catholic Church?
4. a) Who tells us about Easter 1916?
   b) What do we learn about the author?
5. a) How is the complexity of the Irish character ("the weasel's tooth, the weasel's twist") reflected by the poem?
   b) Find a couple of phrases to illustrate the above statement!
6. In what way does the poet support the view "a terrible beauty is born"?
7. In what way do the headlines from two recent newspaper articles on Northern Ireland echo the line from Yeat's poem? In what way are they different?
   The Guardian, February 22, 1975: "A terrible ugliness is born":
   The Observer, February 6, 1972: "A terrible hatred is born".
8. How does the illustration correspond with the poem? Explain!

The Partition of Ireland (1920)

The loyal Protestants in the North looked even more precious than before; and the British Government grew prepared to see Ireland divided rather than lose them altogether.
The Sunday Times, January 13, 1974

That idea, partition, was the one finally adopted by the Lloyd George Coalition in the Government of Ireland Act in December 1920, and ratified in the Treaty talks with the Republican leaders a year later. The United Kingdom was to keep the north-eastern corner of the island, where the Protestants predominated: the rest of it was to go free.

The limitations on that freedom, although the new Republic fought a civil war about them, were all peacefully removed within 30 years. The abiding problem about partition proved to be the actual line of the border. The Act drew it, temporarily, where it runs still. The Treaty proposed a boundary commission to fix it definitely; and the South's negotiators were confident that the commission would give them two whole Ulster counties – Fermanagh and Tyrone – and parts of three more. But first the new administration in the North refused to make an appointment to the commission, and then the views of the British-appointed chairman (a South African judge) proved so conservative that the South's man withdrew too. The border stayed unchanged.

(J. Whale, loc. cit.)

Charles Craig, brother of Sir James Craig, the Northern Premier, put it like this in 1920: "The three excluded counties contain some 70,000 Unionists and some 260,000 Sinn Feiners and Nationalists, and the addition of that large bloc of Sinn Feiners and Nationalists would reduce our majority to such a level that no sane man would undertake to carry on a parliament with it". (Parliamentary Debates: Official Report [Hansard] House of Commons, Vol. 127, Col. 990-1)

(Farrell, p. 366–7)

So the Protestants were left not with a four-county area where Catholics would be so few as to be unthreatening, nor yet with a nine-county area (the old province of Ulster) where Catholics would be numerous enough to provide a normal opposition and perhaps even a government, but with a six-county stake-out which was the largest the Protestants felt they could hold. It was what their leaders in the Unionist Party wanted; but their majority over-all was not impregnable, and in places it was nonexistent.

To maintain control, in consequence, they found it necessary to gerrymander electoral boundaries within the new province, and to counteract the slightly higher Catholic birthrate by showing Catholics good reason to emigrate. This took the form of police bullying backed by special legislative powers, and of making it more than ordinarily difficult for Catholics to get jobs or public housing. It was the eighteenth-century system of penal laws against Catholics even less pardonably renewed. Fermanagh County Council was the admiration of Protestant Ulster for the way it ran its affairs. Its cunningly-drawn electoral boundaries converted a slender Catholic majority in the county as a whole into a steady two-to-one Protestant majority in the council chamber; and that majority was used to give Protestants an advantage of more than two to one in public housing, and more than eight to one in public jobs. The arrangement persisted well into the 1960s. According to a calculation made in 1969, out of 370 posts with Fermanagh County Council no fewer than 332, including all the top ones, were filled at that time by Protestants. To such mean tyranny had these upholders of the light of freedom come. . . .

(J. Whale, loc. cit.)

Notes on the text:

partition: dividing a country into parts

to predominate: have control over, be superior in numbers and influence

the abiding problem: never-ending problem

temporarily: lasting for a short short time only

boundary commission: group of experts set up for discussing and deciding upon the final line of the border

refused to make an appointment: they didn't join the commission

conservative: here: moderate, avoiding extremes (dt. vorsichtig)

Sinn Feiners: Sinn Fein = political party founded in Ireland in 1907 as a separatist but not Republican party. It was infiltrated by the Irish Republican Brotherhood and after 1916 became the main voice of militant Republicanism.

unthreatening: to be not dangerous

a six-county stake-out: Northern Ireland consists of six counties compared with nine counties in the ancient province of Ulster (to stake out = mark an area with stakes (= piece of metal or wood) in order to claim that area)

impregnable: sth that can't be defeated

to gerrymander electoral boundaries: to manipulate the boundaries of constituencies (dt. Manipulation bei der Einteilung der Wahlkreise) cf. Extra Material p. 67–69

police bullying: frightening or hurting those who are weaker by using one's strength or power

less pardonably: sth which can't be excused

persisted into the 1960s: continued to exist until the 1960s

What you have to do

Guided Analysis
Essay

Guided Analysis

Before writing a coherent analysis answer the following questions first.

Use the maps, the statistical figures and the information and phrases from the text.

These will help you to write a coherent analysis of "The Partition of Ireland in 1920", explaining in detail

- the political situation which led to the idea of partition
- the groups involved and their political aims
- the various concepts of partition put forward
- the reasons for the actual line of the border as drawn in 1920
- the abiding consequences of the partition up to the present day

Answer the following questions:

1. What effects did the First World War and the Easter Rising 1916 have on Britain's attitude towards Ireland?
2. Which moods and movements were strengthened among the Irish population in the South and in the North?
3. There were three main political forces involved in Ireland at that time: the Nationalists with their stronghold in the South, the Unionists with their stronghold in the North, and Britain. What were their aims?
4. Look at the results of the 1918 General Election in Great Britain and Ireland:

1918

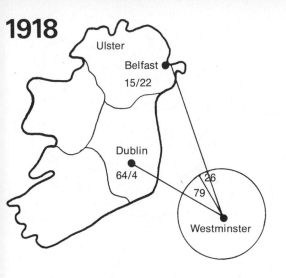

General Election 1918

Results
Ireland (all 32 counties)

Sinn Fein and
Nationalist Party
79   Members of Parliament
64   Leinster, Munster, Connacht
15   Ulster

Unionist Party
26   Members of Parliament
22   Ulster
 4   Dublin

5. Why were the Unionists in the North not interested at all in an independent Ireland with one parliament in Dublin?

6. Let's now look at the various concepts of partion:

   a) Why did the Ulster Unionists and Britain not keep the nine-county area of the historical province of Ulster as a whole?

Outline map of the historical province of Ulster before 1920

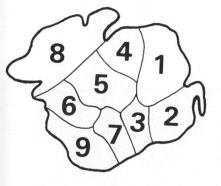

Counties	1918 General Election Results	
1 = Antrim		
2 = Down		
3 = Armagh		56,3% Unionists
4 = Derry		
5 = Tyrone	= 55.4% Nationalists	
6 = Fermanagh	= 56.2% Nationalists	43,7% Nationalists
7 = Monaghan	= 74.7% Nationalists	
8 = Donegal	= 78.9% Nationalists	
9 = Cavan	= 81.5% Nationalists	

(Figures from: Farrell, p. 24)

b) Why did the Ulster Unionists not content themselves with a four-county area? Which of the two arguments appears to be more convincing to you:
   - in a four-county area Catholics would have been so few as to be unthreatening
   - a four-county area would have been physically, strategically and economically unviable and would have involved abandoning another 90,000 Protestants to the South

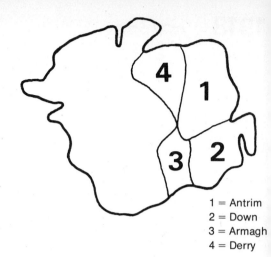

1 = Antrim
2 = Down
3 = Armagh
4 = Derry

c) What advantages did the six-county area provide for the Unionists?

Outline map of Northern Ireland after the partition in December 1920

Counties	1918 General election Results
1 = Antrim	
2 = Down	
3 = Armagh	66% Unionists
4 = Derry	
5 = Tyrone	34% Nationalists
6 = Fermanagh	

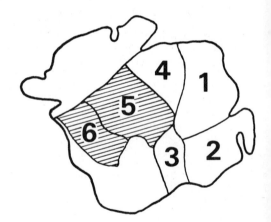

7. Why is 1920 such an important date in the history of "The Troubles" in Northern Ireland?

Essay

Write now a short essay (about 200 words) on
"The Partition of Ireland in 1920"

Extra material

"Gerrymandering"

Word definition

to gerrymander: manipulate boundaries of (constituency etc.) unfairly so as to secure disproportionate influence at election for some party or class (orig. U. S., by substitution of name of governor Gerry of Massachusetts [1812] for sala- in mander)
(The Concise Oxford Dictionary, 1976)

The Official Report

229. Having carried out as full an investigation as lay within our competence we can summarise our conclusions upon the immediate and precipitating causes of the disorders which broke out in Londonderry on 5th October 1968 and continued thereafter both in Londonderry and elsewhere on subsequent dates. These are both general and particular ...

(3) Complaints, again well documented, in some cases of deliberate manipulation of local government electoral boundaries and in others a refusal to apply for their necessary extension, in order to achieve and maintain Unionist control of local authorities and so to deny to Catholics influence in local government proportionate to their numbers (paragraphs 133–137). *(Disturbances in Northern Ireland Report of the Commission appointed by the Governor of Northern Ireland, Belfast, HMSO, September 1969, Cmd. 532, p. 91)*

Local elections in 1920

... the six-county area created problems. Though it had a Protestant majority of 820,000 to 430,000 this was not evenly distributed. Two whole counties, Fermanagh and Tyrone, had Catholic majorities of 56.2 per cent and 55.4 per cent respectively, and the second city of the area, Derry, had a Catholic majority of 56.2 per cent as well. There were also overwhelmingly Catholic areas in South Armagh and South Down, including the town of Newry, and even in Belfast there was a strongly Catholic enclave concentrated on the Falls Road in West Belfast ...

The results were seen in January and June 1920 when local elections were held throughout Ireland, using proportional representation (PR)

for the first time. PR was introduced to reduce the power of Sinn Fein in the South of Ireland; but in the North it had the effect of giving greater representation to non-Unionists. In the six-county area Nationalists won control of Derry City, Fermanagh and Tyrone County Councils, ten urban councils, including Armagh, Omagh, Enniskillen, Newry and Strabane, and thirteen rural councils. It was the first serious challenge to Unionist hegemony in the area. The Derry City result was crucial.

Derry held a central place in Orange mythology. Its walled town was built by the planters in 1614. It held out for the Protestant William of Orange in 1688–90 against the Catholic King James II. It was still very much a plantation town with its Protestant walled citadel perched on a hill overlooking the sprawling Catholic township of the Bogside which had grown up on the marshy ground outside the walls. The Corporation of Derry had been Protestant-controlled since the great siege in 1688 and careful *gerrymandering* had kept it that way despite a growing Catholic majority in the city. Now for the first time in 230 years the city had a Catholic and Nationalist corporation and mayor ...

The effect on the Loyalists of Derry was traumatic. *(Farrell, p. 24–25)*

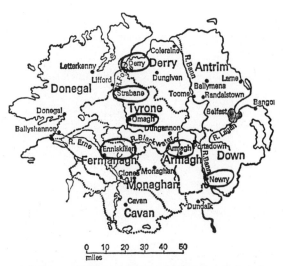

2. Outline map of Ulster showing some places mentioned in the text. The counties of Donegal, Cavan and Monaghan are in the Republic of Ireland.

Control of local government was to be handed over from Dublin Castle to the Belfast government on 21 December 1921..." "In July 1922" a "Local Government Bill was introduced to abolish proportional representation (PR) in local elections and make a declaration of allegiance to the Crown and government obligatory on all councillors. It was rushed through parliament because further elections were due in 1923, and with the Boundary Commission looming over them the government couldn't afford another round of Nationalist victories. However the British government was embarrassed at such a prompt attempt to remove one of the safeguards they had introduced for minorities North and South, and for the first – and last – time the Royal Assent to the Bill was withheld for a few months.

When the Bill became law the job was only half done. The local boundaries had still to be redrawn and the elections had to be postponed till 1924...

William Miller, Unionist MP for Fermanagh and Tyrone, was able to boast on... 12 July (1923): "When the government of Northern Ireland decided to do away with proportional representation the chance that they had been waiting for for so long arrived and they took advantage of it ... they divided the country in the way they thought best.

Local elctions in 1924

The immediate result was devastating. After the elections in 1924 Nationalists controlled only two out of nearly 80 local councils in the North, compared with 25 in 1920...

In the two Catholic-majority counties of Fermanagh and Tyrone the Nationalists had lost the county councils and every single rural council. In Fermanagh they controlled nothing; in Tyrone only Strabane and Omagh Urban Councils.

Some of the results were bizarre. In the Omagh Rural Council area, with a 61.5 per cent Catholic majority, the Nationalists had won the council in 1920 with 26 seats to 13. After Leech's (a one-man Judicial Commission to fix the new boundaries) endeavours the Unionists held it with 21 seats to 18. Magherafelt Rural Council had had a Nationalist majority of 17 to 11. After 1924 it had a Unionist majority of 18 to 11. And the *gerrymandering* didn't stop in 1924. It was a continuous process ...

The technique of gerrymandering

The technique involved in all this was simple but effective. In areas with a Nationalist majority the wards were so drawn that Nationalist seats were won with huge majorities, thus "wasting" Nationalist votes, while Unionist majorities were small but adequate. The process was aided by the restricted franchise – limited to rate-payers and their wives – which discriminated against the poorer Catholic population; by the virtually complete identification of religion and political views; and by the high degree of religious segregation even in rural areas.

e.g. Derry City

Probably the clearest example of gerrymandering at work was Derry City. In 1966 the adult population of Derry was 30,376 – 20,102 Catholics and 10,274 Protestants – yet the Corporation was still Unionist-controlled.

First the restricted franchise reduced the Catholic majority substantially, to 14,429 Catholics to 8,781 Protestants. Second, after constant boundary revisions the city was divided into three wards as follows:

(Farrell, p. 82–84)

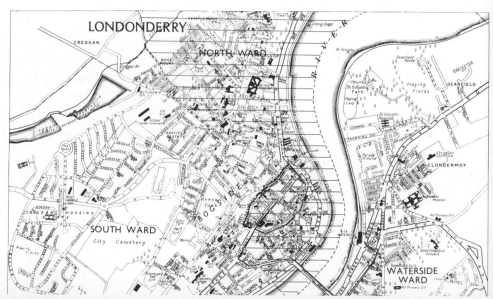

Londonderry County Borough (1967)

	Catholic Voters	Other Voters	Seats
North Ward	2,530	3,946	8 Unionists
Waterside Ward	1,852	3,697	4 Unionists
South Ward	10,047	1,138	8 Non-Unionists
Total:	14,429	8,781	20
	23,210		

(Disturbances in Northern Ireland, Report of the Commission, appointed by the Governor of Northern Ireland [Cameron Report], HMSO, Belfast 1969, Cmd. 532, p. 59, para. 134)

Eventually the Nationalists were left in control only of those areas where the Catholic majority was so large that no gerrymandering could do away with it. They included only two towns of any importance: Newry and Strabane. The effects of the gerrymander were also permanent. No council which became Unionist as a result of it was ever re-captured by the Nationalists, and they soon gave up trying. Local elections became foregone conclusions and the bulk of the seats were left uncontested . . .

The gerrymandering process went on right up to 1967 . . .

The effects of the local government gerrymandering were far-reaching. Immediately it strengthened the Northern government's position before the Boundary Commission. As far as the Catholic minority were concerned it sharpened their sense of grievance. They were paying the price of defeat. And it deprived them of power even in the areas where they were in a majority, most notably in Derry. It seemed there was no place for them in the new state.

But control of local government was of more than symbolic significance. Local councils controlled the building and allocating of public housing and appointment to hundreds — later thousands — of jobs which were vitally important in an area of high unemployment, bad housing, and emigration. Unionist control of local government even in Nationalist areas, could deprive Catholics of jobs and houses and give local Unionist or Orange bosses a powerful source of patronage to use to keep their Protestant supporters loyal.

(Farrell, p. 82–86)

What you have to do

Prepare a speech (teamwork)

Prepare a speech (teamwork):

"How the Protestants in Ulster managed to construct a Protestant state with almost all political power in their own hands"

Refer to the following aspects:
- the political problems the six-county area created in terms of local elections
- how the Northern government dealt with these problems
- the technique of gerrymandering Londonderry as the classic example of gerrymandering
- the effects of the Belfast government's policy on the Catholic minority

Comment on the following statement:
"The overall effect on the Catholic population was to make them despair. Many of them had been attacked, terrorised and driven from their homes. They had been cut off from the rest of Ireland and forced into a state run by their enemies. Now they were deprived of political power, discriminated against and driven on to the dole or the emigrant boat. (cf. though only one third of the population, Catholics provided the bulk of those on the emigrant boat – 90,000 out of 159,000 who emigrated between 1937 and 1961).

They were soon to find that if they put their trust in politicians their representatives met with no response. It was inevitable that some would turn to violence."

(Farrell, p. 92,

Part 3:
The troubles in
Northern Ireland

Why the troubles began (1960s)

A much larger Catholic middle-class has emerged, which is less ready to acquiesce in the acceptance of a situation of assumed (or established) inferiority and discrimination than was the case in the past. This is, we think, an important and new element in the political and social climate of Northern Ireland and has played its part in the events (= violence and civil disturbance on and since 5th October 1968 in Londonderry, Armagh, Newry, Dungannon, Enniskillen) which led to the setting up of this Enquiry. We were impressed by the number of well educated and responsible people who were and are concerned in, and have taken an active part in, the Civil Rights movement.

Disturbances in Northern Ireland: Report of the Commission appointed by the Governor of Northern Ireland (Cameron Report) HMSO, Belfast, September 1969, p. 15, par. 11

"Settler régimes"

Historically, the problems created by oppressive settler régimes have for the most part been resolved either by the total victory of the settlers, as in the United States, or (more often) by their departure, as in the former Belgian Congo. By 1962 even the Algerian *pieds noirs,* the most limpet-like colonists of modern times, were on the boats home. But in Northern Ireland nothing changed. The need to defend Britain remained paramount. 1962 was also the year when a Russia missile threat to the United States was held to be infinitely more dangerous from Cuba than if it had come from mainland Russia. Off-shore islands were still a high security risk. Then again, there was no pressure for change from Northern Ireland Catholics. In 1962 the IRA abandoned a sporadic border campaign for lack, confessedly, of popular support.

"The world changed"

Yet change came, within a decade. The world changed. The gradual advance towards Western European unity meant that France and Germany (let alone Spain) became each year less believable as countries that might attack Britain again. The further development of the ballistic missile meant that even if they did—even if Russia or China did – they would scarcely need to go round by way of Ireland. (The Russian intercontinental system was largely in place by the end of 1965.)

The world changed in another way, too. The whole notion of equality of opportunity, of the right of every human being to certain minimum benefits, had a new airing. In Northern Ireland, the fierce reaction to that idea produced in time a counter-reaction: the IRA Provisionals.

"The movement for Catholic civil rights"

Influenced by the ferment of the Kennedy presidency in the United States, the movement for Catholic civil rights began in Northern Ireland in 1963. A Dungannon doctor's wife pressed the local council on Catholic housing. She had some success. At the same time Terence O'Neill, the new Prime Minister, set out on a path of guarded acknowledgment that Catholics in the North and the Catholic state in the South did at any rate exist.

"Violent Protestant reaction"

To both trends the reaction of many stern-minded Protestants was disproportionately and self-destroyingly violent. They foresaw the loss of the separate and unequal status fostered by Britain for 350 years. Egged on by the men who lead them still, Ian Paisley and William Craig, they identified the Civil Rights Association with the IRA. They were wrong at the time (the authority is the 1969 Cameron Report); but they made their identification come true.

Catholic civil rights marches in the winter of 1968–69 were met with physical assault by Protestants, not least those in the ranks of the regular and auxiliary police forces. The worst incidents were at Derry and Burntollet. Angrier protests brought fiercer suppression. (...) *(J. Whale, loc. cit.)*

The official Report

177. We have to record with regret that our investigations have led us to the unhesitating conclusion that on the night of 4th/5th January a number of policemen were guilty of misconduct which involved assault and battery, malicious damage to property in streets in the predominantly Catholic Bogside area giving reasonable cause for apprehension of personal injury among other innocent inhabitants, and the use of provocative sectarian and political slogans. While we fully realize that the police had been working without adequate relief or rest for long hours, and were under great stress, we are afraid that not only do we find these allegations of misconduct are substantiated, but that for such conduct among members of a disciplined and well-led force there can be no acceptable justification or excuse. We have also considered the full and careful Report of County Inspector Baillie which has been made available to us (and whose evidence we heard) and we note, with some satisfaction, though with regret, that his independent investigation has led him to reach the same conclusions as to the gravity and nature of the misconduct as those at which we have arrived in our consideration of the evidence before us. Although this unfortunate and temporary breakdown of discipline was limited in extent, its effect in rousing passions and inspiring hostility towards the police was regrettably great, and obscure the restraint, under conditions of severe strain, then displayed by the large majority of the police concerned. *(Report of the Commission appointed by the Governor of Northern Ireland (Cameron Report) Belfast: HMSO 1969, p. 73)*

Notes on the text:

to acquiesce in s.th.: to agree to accept s.th. without protest

assumed (or established) inferiority: impression/belief or actual situation of being lower in rank, social position or quality

oppressive settler régimes: government of settlers (in colonies) ruling the country and population in a hard and cruel way. (e.g. the *pieds noirs* in the former French colony of Algeria)

limpet: (fig.) person who sticks tightly to a position, office or another person, derived from limpet = small shell fish that fastens itself tightly to rocks.

to remain paramount: (formal) to keep on being pre-eminent, most important.

Russian missile threat: the situation in 1962 when Russia had been allowed to have missiles in Cuba in return for economic and financial aid for Castro's Cuba.

ballistic missile: rocket with a warhead.

the notion of equality of opportunity: the concept/idea of every human being having the right of certain minimum benefits and chances.

to have a new airing: to sound or look new and interesting; (here:) to be discussed publicly under new aspects and with new interest

the ferment of the Kennedy Presidency: (fig.) new and exciting impulse or impetus resulting from the new. U.S. President, J. F. Kennedy.

he set out on a path of: (formal) he started doing s.th. (slowly and/or carefully)

guarded acknowledgement: admitting or confessing cautiously

stern-minded: holding strict or severe views of s.th., strict, inflexible attitude.

disproportionately and self-destroyingly violent: (a reaction) so inadequately violent and out of proportion that it was damaging (to the Protestants)

(a status) fostered by Britain: supported, cared for by Britain

they were egged on: they were urged (to do s.th.)

they were met with physical assault: (formal) they were attacked violently

auxiliary police force: voluntary policemen to help the regular police; in Northern Ireland: set up by Protestants against Catholics

unhesitating conclusion: immediate and direct c., without having to think or to discuss about it for long.

they were guilty of misconduct: they had done wrong, behaved badly

assault and battery: (bodily) attacks and beating

malicious damage: d. done on purpose, in order to harm or intimidate s.o.

apprehension: fear

allegations of s.th.: reports, information about

to substantiate s.th.: to show that s.th. is true, to give facts/examples to support or prove s.th.

gravity: (here) weight, seriousness

its effect in rousing passions and inspiring hostility: people were very excited about it and got angry about, and unfriendly to, the police

to obscure s.th.: to make s.th. disappear, to hide s.th.

restraint: self-control

severe strain: very strong demands on o.'s strength; stress, hardship

to display: to show, demonstrate

What you have to do

Questions on the text

Read the text carefully and answer the following questions:

1. What happened to two settler régimes in the early sixties?
2. Was their fate unusual?
3. What has been happening to such régimes in Africa since then?
4. Can you see a pattern in the recent developments in the Third World?
5. Was it for a) cultural, b) economic, c) political, or d) strategic reasons, according to the text, that no change took place in Ulster up to 1962?
6. Can you quote an earlier title or phrase to support your choice in question 5?
7. State the two developments which changed the status quo in Ulster.
8. Was there a single attitude among the Protestants towards these developments?
9. How were the Catholics organized?
10. How many groups did the Protestant leaders distinguish among the Catholics?
11. What was typical of the Protestant counter-demonstrations?
12. What role did the police play in those clashes?

Guided summary

Write a summary of about 120 words to answer the key question: "Why did the troubles in Northern Ireland begin in the late 1960s?" Use your answers (to question 1–12) as a basis for your summary!

Version

Translate the first paragraph ("Settler régimes") into German

Comment

Write a short comment (appr. 120 words) dealing with the following points:

What are the reasons – according to Mrs Claxton – why the troubles started in Northern Ireland in the late sixties?
Do you agree with the analysis given in the text or do you think the author fails to mention important reasons?

Background to the troubles: The late sixties

UNFORTUNATELY neither the government nor the churches did much to bridge the gap. Catholicism remained identified with Irish Nationalism. Protestantism remained identified with Unionism. This was the situation in 1965 when the then Unionist Prime Minister of Northern Ireland, Terence O'Neill, met the Republican Prime Minister Sean Lemass for discussions. Although O'Neill was careful to stress that constitutional and political issues had not been discussed, the powerful right-wing extremist group in his own party bitterly resented the meeting, and no further progress was possible. In 1969 O'Neill retired from active politics, a bitter and disillusioned man.

The failure of O'Neill and of moderate Unionism was partly due to the rise of the Rev. Ian Paisley, a loud-mouthed self-made preacher of an illiberal and extremist sect. While O'Neill was attempting to mediate – an attempt which at that time still had possibilities of success – Paisley was thanking God that "the 1916 rebellion was a failure and that Ulster is still free from Papal tyranny". At first he was regarded as a joke. But unfortunately as an orator and a ruthless politician he was able to play upon the fears of many Protestants who really believed that any gesture towards Catholics would lead to the Papal domination of Northern Ireland. Paisley and Paisleyism became one of the most divisive forces in Ulster society at a time when not only relations with the Free State but those between the groups within the six counties might have improved.

Young Catholics, impatient with the lack of government action, formed a new Civil Rights Association. The issue exploded into international prominence when marchers were batoned and drenched by water cannon by the police in Londonderry on October 5, 1968, in full view of the press and television cameras. For the next seven years the Civil Rights supporters continued their demonstrations, provoking Protestant counter-demonstrations (. . .)

Extract from:
World and Press. 1st September 1976. Carol M. Claxton: Background to the Troubles. A short history of Ireland in two part.

Text & Style

Let's have a look at the language used in a newspaper article (cf. quotations from J. Whale's "The end of a long story . . ." Sunday Times, January 13, 1974)

1. The author uses brackets four times in this short passage:

. . . or *(more often)* by their departure . . .

. . . that France and Germany *(let alone Spain)* become . . .

. . . *(The Russian intercontinental . . . by the end of 1965).*

. . . at the time *(the authority . . . Report);*
How do these visual signals work?
What is the function of these brackets in each instance?
Discuss its effects in class!

2. The stylistic structure of language: How to do things with words (Or: How to express the same thing in different ways)

Have a look at the language of the newspaper article. Try and express the following quotations in ordinary every-day English (active/passive voice)!

"(. . .) O'Neill, the new Prime Minister, set out on a path of guarded acknowledgment that Catholics in the North and the Catholic state in the South did at any rate exist."

"(. . .) Then again, there was no pressure for change from Northern Ireland Catholics. In 1962 the IRA abandoned a sporadic border campaign for lack, confessedly, of popular support."

76

You will notice that you can replace these complicated expressions by simple verbs. They are typical examples of the so-called "nominal style".

Have a look at the passages from the Government Report.

Can you find similar stylistic devices in the report?

"We have to record with regret that our investigations have led us to the unhesitating conclusion that on the night of 4th–5th January (1969) a num- ber of policemen were guilty of misconduct which involved assault and battery, (. . .)"

"(. . .) giving reasonable cause for apprehension of personal injury among other innocent inhabitants . . .

For such conduct among members of a disciplined and well-led force there can be no acceptable justification or excuse."

(Cameron Report, p. 73, par. 177)

Are there more of these devices in the report than in the newspaper text?

3. Compare the statement of the Government Report to the report of an eyewitness:

I just couldn't take in what was happening. I saw a policeman raise his baton to a young girl and I stood there paralysed in front of him. There must have been horror on my face because he lowered his baton and walked away.

After that my faith in the police was shaken. I continued to go on the civil rights marches, and there was I, always on peaceful demonstrations and they were always kicking the tripes out of me.

("How the IRA gained a sniper" The Observer, February 6, 1972)

What are both reports about?

How "close" are these reports to the events?

Characterize the authors' attitudes towards their subject matters!

4. Look at the three texts again and compare their style!

Decide which style has which characteristics!

☐ abstract

☐ formal

☐ distant

☐ concrete/realistic

☐ lively/narrative/descriptive

☐ close

Try and characterize the intended effect on the reader of these texts!

☐ neutral information

☐ critical distance

☐ irony

☐ understatement

☐ covering up

☐ careful balancing of views

☐ apologetic, justifying the events

British Policy in Ulster 1969-1972: Military Intervention

. . . a further burden: the presence of a large and growing army . . . British soldiers were bound to be more in Catholic areas than Protestant: the Protestants were their friends, and needed little watching. But an army is not a police force.

(J. Whale loc. cit.)

August 1969: British troops moved in

By August 1969 after a Northern Ireland general election and a change of prime minister had settled nothing, fighting between the two communities had passed well beyond police control. British troops stationed outside Derry and Belfast moved in to keep them from each other's throats.

A parcel of reforms purporting to free Catholics from discrimination, and competently imposed on a bewildered Ulster Cabinet by James Callaghan as the Wilson Government's Home Secretary, left the central problem untouched: that in a state designed – but clumsily designed – as an enclave garrisoned by Protestants for the British, Irish Catholics could have no sense of valued participation, no object for their pride or loyalty as citizens. Now they had a further burden: the presence of a large and growing army in their streets.

British soldiers were bound to be more in Catholic areas than Protestant: the Protestants were their friends, and needed little watching. But an army is not a police force. For as long as Labour stayed in power, natural military zeal in searching houses and controlling rioters was checked and held back.

June 1970: "The hood came off the falcon"

The Conservative tradition, back in force after June 1970, was to let the Army get on with the job in its own way. The hood came off the falcon.

Other persuasions had their weight in the resurgence of armed republicanism (including money paid by the governing party in the South as an inducement to activists to confine their activities to the North): but it was at bottom as a response to the Army's altered methods – "an animal reaction," one Belfast Catholic MP called it – that the old IRA spawned its militant offspring, the Provisionals.

The first British soldiers lost their lives in February 1971. The cycle of violence was gathering pace.

August 1971: internment was introduced

The Westminster Government allowed one Ulster Prime Minister (James Chichester-Clark) to fall because he wanted too much Army intervention: he was replaced by a man who wanted more and got it. Brian Faulkner's panacea was to have republicans interned. Once internment was introduced in August 1971, and the affront to Catholics compounded by the cruel questioning of certain prisoners, recruitment to the Provisionals climbed dizzily.

It is still too early to make a judgment of internment. Indefinite imprisonment without trial was not much of an addition to the quality of life in the United Kingdom; but the British had long been used to behaving by different standards in Ireland. Internment put more Provisionals on the streets than it took off; but at least the men lately released may conceivably have cooled towards militancy during their long wait in the muddy compounds of Long Kesh.

"The interminable alternation of violence and counter-violence"

At the time, internment was simply one more episode in the interminable alternation of violence and counter-violence. It provoked the Provisionals to a new ferocity. In the four months before it began, four soldiers were killed and four civilians. In the four months which followed, the dead numbered 41 members of the forces of order and 73 civilians.

As one result working-class Protestants began to band together in conscious imitation of the IRA. They had no educated leadership, contrary to widespread belief, no intelligence and no strategy. As another result, the mailed hand of the British Army fell with ever-increasing weight on Catholics in general.

Derry, 30 January 1972 "Bloody Sunday"

The end was the carnage which followed a banned anti-internment march in Derry on Bloody Sunday. In a battalion operation not clearly authorised at brigade level, disapproved by the police, and begun when other methods of keeping order seemed to be succeeding. British troops used rifles and used them carelessly. At least five of the 13 dead were killed without justification. That much was later established in a report on the incident by the Lord Chief Justice of England, Lord Widgery. . . . .

(J. Whale, loc. cit.)

Notes on the text:

to settle: (here:) to decide, to

fighting had passed well beyond police control: the police could not prevent or control the fights any more.

to keep them from each other's throat: to prevent them from fighting (or killing) each other.

purporting: intending, seeming to mean, claiming.

competently imposed on s.o.: forced on s.o. in a clever and diligent way

bewildered: surprised

enclave: (separate) territory within the boundaries of another.

valued: important, meaningful, regarded highly.

hood: (here:) small cap on a falcon's head to prevent him from seeing and flying off.

persuasion: (here:) belief, conviction

resurgence: revival

the old IRA spawned its offsprings: the old IRA produced a new IRA group (offspring = children)

the Provisionals: cf. glossary

his panacea was to have republicans interned: his remedy for all troubles and problems was internment of republicans.

compounded: increased, completed

conceivably: (adv. of) conceivable, easy to understand/imagine, seeming possible or likely.

to cool towards s.th.: to lose interest in s.th., not to like s.th. any longer.

the muddy compounds of Long Kesh: the dirty and wet camp of L.K. (a former British airfield in Northern Ireland, used as prison for suspected members of the IRA)

the mailed hand/(fist): (fig. use of a military term from the Middle Ages, meaning:) military power, physical force.

carnage: blood bath, killing of many people.

Lord Chief Justice: judge of the Supreme Court.

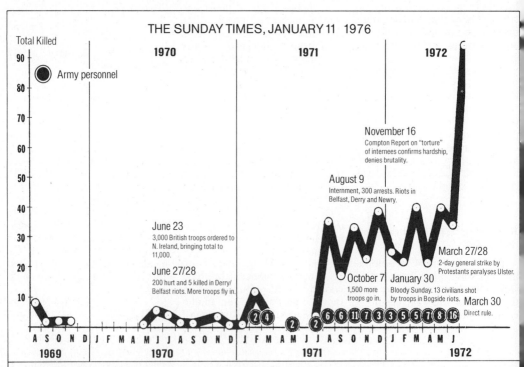

THE SUNDAY TIMES, JANUARY 11 1976

The violent pattern of Ulster: the black graph line shows the total number of deaths in each month since troops were sent in. The circled figures represent army deaths alone.

What you have to do

Questions on the text
Guided analysis

Questions on the text

Read the text carefully and answer the following questions briefly:

1. Were there any political or personal changes after the general election at the end of the sixties?
2. What relationship was left untouched by the anti-discrimination acts imposed by the British Home Secretary?
3. What did the Conservative Government in 1970 believe in?
4. What demands were made by the Ulster Government?
5. What effect did internment have on the attitude of the Catholic community towards the Provisionals?
6. How did the Provos react towards the other side?
7. What pattern does internment fit in?
8. How did Protestant workers answer the Provisionals' actions?
9. Describe briefly the character of their organization!
10. How many groups were involved in the Bloody Sunday events?

Guided analysis

The Army's job in Ulster August 1969–January 1972

Assess the aims, the measures, and the effects of British policy in Northern Ireland between 1969 and 1972! Use the following questions as a guide line for your analysis (100–150 words).

1. What was the British Army's task when they moved in in 1969?
2. Where they successful in this? (Look at the graphs!)
3. Was it possible for them, and were they able to play their original role in Ulster in the long run?
4. How and why did the Army's role change in the course of events (esp. in 1970)?
5. Point out the immediate effects of the Army's measures and actions (using the figures given in the graph!)
6. How and why was the "cycle of violence" gathering pace?
7. "Internment": Explain shortly what this term means – in the Ulster context.
8. If you look at the figures in the graphs: would you say internment served its purpose? Describe its effects in terms of casualties!
9. Try and find some reasons for its adverse effects.

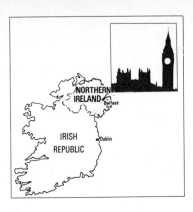

British Policy in Ulster 1972-1978 Direct Rule

For four years and more, it has been British policy in Northern Ireland to hold the fort till reconciliation dawns. The idea has been that the Army will gradually put down violence, and in the safer climate thus created the two communities will agree on a new shared administration whose policemen will then replace the soldiers. To a good many people, of whom I have been one, it has seemed the most humane and responsible course open.

The policy has one grave flaw. It has not worked, and shows no sign of working.

(The Sunday Times, October 30, 1976)

30th March 1972
Direct Rule

Within two months, and without waiting for Widgery, the British Government had cancelled the Lloyd George settlement. On March 30, 1972, Northern Ireland's separate parliament was suspended. Not just 50 but 350 years of British policy in Ireland were reversed. Released by Europe from the strategic preoccupation, repelled by the endless squalid killings which the old policy was at last seen to entail, the British were no longer backing the Protestants. Heath spelt it out in terms which have been made good: Catholics, too, were to have an "active, permanent and guaranteed role in the life and public affairs of the Province.

Where the Provisionals were wrong

The Provisionals believed that it was solely their military action which had changed British minds thus far, and they believed that more of the same would change them farther, and in the end Protestant minds too. They ignored the shift in Britain's strategic need. They forgot that violence only has a chance of succeeding when it touches a nerve of guilt (and not always then): it dislodged President Batista in Cuba, but it could do nothing for Quebec separatism. They made the mistake which General Tanganyika of Mau Mau made in Kenya, and General Grivas of Eoka in Cyprus, in the 1950s. By persisting beyond the point where there were political dividends to be won, they missed their chance to cash their cheque.

The Orange flag revived

As the green flag drooped, the Orange flag revived. While the Provisionals were throwing away their political and military authority, violent Protestant groups were re-establishing their presence. By the autumn of 1972, twice as many Catholics as Protestants were falling victim to sly, sectarian assassination. Yet that was not the main reason why British ministers, who had been briefly tempted by the idea of dumping the Protestants, now turned to the aim of reconciling them to a new status instead.

The fact was that policy could at last be governed by considerations of ordinary fairness. The Protestants were the problem, and it was in origin Britain's fault that they were there. But the present generation of Protestants could not help being there and to pretend that they were not there – although it had been the myopic treatment which they had themselves meted out to Catholics – would only shift the burden of unfairness to a different set of shoulders.

(John Whale, loc. cit.)

British policy in Northern Ireland: to hold the fort till reconciliation dawns

For four years and more, it has been British policy in Northern Ireland to hold the fort till reconciliation dawns. The idea has been that the Army will gradually put down violence, and in the safer climate thus created the two communities will agree on a new shared administration whose policemen will then replace the soldiers. To a good many people, of whom I have been one, it has seemed the most humane and responsible course open.

Till the crack of doom

The policy has one grave flaw. It has not worked, and shows no sign of working. Not even the surge of feeling represented by the Peace People has saved it. Unless policy changes, British troops will be in Northern Ireland till the crack of doom.

Violence is not being put down. British soldiers have shown sustained bravery and skill; yet the Provisional IRA retains the power to hit them hard.

From self-interest to disinterest

Britain's reputation abroad suffers: sometimes justly, as in the recent findings of the Strasbourg court; sometimes unjustly, as in the stream of ignorant abuse poured out by Irish-Americans.

That might be bearable if we could get the thing right in the end. But there is no sign that we can. We are as lost as we have always been. We have mismanaged our dealings with the island of Ireland for 800 years; and although our motive has changed in the past decade from self-interest to dis-interest, the world does not perceive it, and neither do most of the Irish. It is an island where we are fated to be misunderstood as much as we misunderstand.

What, then, can be done?

(John Whale, The Sunday Times,
October 30, 1976)

The violent pattern of Ulster 1972–1975
The Sunday Times, January 11, 1976

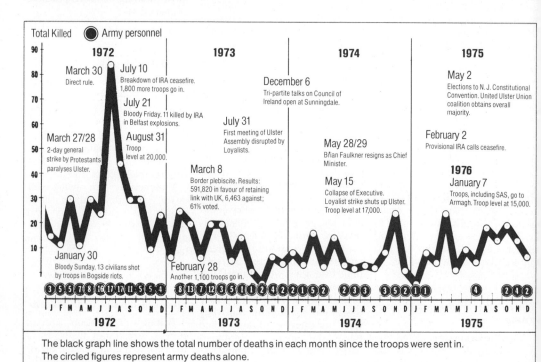

The black graph line shows the total number of deaths in each month since the troops were sent in.
The circled figures represent army deaths alone.

Notes on the text:

reconciliation: overcoming hostility between the two communities (in Ulster)

grave flaw: a serious fault

Lloyd George settlement: Government of Ireland Act December 1920, establishing the semi-autonomous status of the Ulster Province with an Ulster Parliament ("Stormont")

released ... from the strategic preoccupation: it was no longer necessary to look at Ireland in military terms

repelled by ... squalid killing: shocked by mean, brutal killing

to entail s.th.: to have as consequence, to cause s.th. to happen

to make good: accomplish what has been tried

the shift in s.th.: change

to dislodge: to remove from a position

Batista: Cuban dictator who was ousted by Castro (1962)

Quebec separatism: regional autonomist movement in French Canada, centred in the city of Quebec.

Mau Mau: black nationalist movement in Kenya against the British colonial regime in the 1950s (important leader: Gen. Tanganyika).

Eoka: Cypriot nationalist underground movement, led by the legendary Gen. Grivas.

cash their cheque: (fig.) to realize o. 's plans

the Green Flag drooped: the hopes of the Irish Republicans faded.

the Orange flag revived: the Protestant Unionists became stronger.

sly, sectarian assassination: members of one community are murdered by members of the other

dumping the Protestants: no longer supporting them militarily and politically

myopic treatment: biased policy, blind to certain facts or problems

till the crack of doom: till the Day of Last Judgement (= bis zum Jüngsten Tage)

Peace People: Women's Peace Movement in Ulster started in August 1976

sustained bravery: lasting courage

findings of the Strasbourg court: (refers to) the established fact of violation of human rights by the British Army in Ulster

84

What you have to do

Version
Questions on the text
Analysing a cartoon
Guided comment

Version

Translate the two short passages "British policy . . ." and "Till the crack of doom"

Questions on the text

1. "30th March 1972. Direct Rule."
   a) Explain shortly: "Not just 50 but 350 years of British policy in Ireland were reversed".
   b) Why – according to the text – did Britain introduce direct rule?
2. "Where the Provisionals were wrong"
   a) Recall the text "Who is fighting whom . . .?" and the passage there on the aims of the Provisional IRA. Why were the Provos interested in the British Government assuming direct rule in Ulster?
   b) Why – according to the text – were the Provos wrong?
   c) What do the historical examples in this passage stand for?
   d) What would have been the "political dividends" the Provos could have won?

3. "The Orange flag revived"
   a) What would have been the result of a British withdrawal in autumn 1972?
   b) How far can you support the author's view that "the Protestants were the problem, and it was in origin Britain's fault that they were there."?
4. "British Policy in Northern Ireland"
   a) What flaw does Britain's policy in Ulster have?
   b) Why did it to "a good many people" seem to be the most humane and responsible course open?
5. "From self-interest to disinterest"
   a) Characterize the author's attitude towards Britain's role in Ireland?
   b) How does the author judge the prospects of Britain's active part in solving the conflict in Northern Ireland?

Analysing a cartoon

1. Answer the following questions:

   Does this type of cartoon remind you of another one in this book?

   How many elements can you distinguish in this cartoon?

   Which elements speak for themselves? Which elements (visual or verbal) are difficult to decode? Explain why!

   The cartoon was published on February 6, 1972. Which event does it refer to?

   Who is to blame for the postponement – according to the cartoonist?

   What is the message of the cartoon? Does it take sides?

2. Summarize your answers in a written analysis of about 120 words!

Guided comment

"How far does the Ulster pattern of violence shown in the graph support the author's view that British policy in Ulster shows no sign of working?"
Have a look at the graph.

The graph provides data of three categories:
years and dates of events
the sides involved
the number of casualties among army personnel and civilians

Use the following questions as a guide line for your comment (about 100 words)
1. What fact leaps to your eye in the chart
2. Do you think there is any link between the dates of events and the number of casualties?
3. Is there any link between the number of troops and the number of casualities?
4. Examine the number of casualities among troops and civilians between 1972 and 1976.

Extra material

The failure of reconciliation

There is no sign of communal reconciliation.
Sectarian strife

Sectarian strife, so far from lessening, grows fiercer. You can see it in the volume of civilian assassinations: Mrs Drumm was the year's 220th victim – the total is already higher than for any year since the full-scale rioting of 1972 – and inevitably not the last.

Steady disappearance of mixed housing areas

You can see it in the steady disappearance of mixed housing areas. In north Belfast, the Catholics have almost gone from the huge estate at Rathcoole; in west Belfast, the Protestants have left Lenadoon altogether and will be gone from Suffolk within two years. A new pattern shows itself: localised partition. An inquiry opened last week into a new estate at Poleglass. If it is built, the Catholic corridor in west Belfast will run all the way from the Lower Falls to Lisburn.

No integrated schools

You can see it – a fresh and revealing piece of evidence, this – in the blank prospects for the movement to have Protestant and Catholic schoolchildren educated together. It has run into a brick wall of Catholic refusal.

The schools example is especially significant. It is a reminder that the sectarian divide in Northern Ireland is deep, and old, and reasoned.

The Catholic refusal.
The Catholic Church in Ireland.

In April 1974 the short-lived coalition Executive decided it could live with shared schools. Backers of the idea were further encouraged, in July of this year, when Merlyn Rees (then Northern Ireland Secretary) showed willingness, at a gathering in Oxford, to set up a conference about it; and in September, when Cardinal Hume (head of the Catholic Church in Britain) said in an unguarded comment to Ludovic Kennedy on BBC television that the argument for integrated schools was "a very strong one."

That argument was clear enough. Old schoolfellows seldom shot each other. Children from either side would learn that representatives of the other side were after all human. Animosities and fears would dwindle.

Yet the light has failed. The opposition of the Catholic Church in Ireland has been flat and final. Its representatives have declined to come to conferences. Its bishops have scouted the idea in public and private.

The important thing about the Catholic refusal is that it is far more than a tribal closing of the ranks. It is rooted in principle. The Catholic Church believes that it alone has hold of the indispensable truths about human life here and hereafter. It therefore wants them taught to its children early, repeatedly, and without the smallest suggestion that they are optional. To do less would be a betrayal. If as a result those children have a hard time when they grow up, that is as nothing in the scale against their immortal salvation.

Even from such schools, the children go back to homes still separated by the basic difference over authority. It extends from belief to conduct. The Catholic Church still reckons to control the content of private lives, from reading matter to methods of birth control. The Protestant mind jibs at that. True religion might well encompass both traditions – authority and autonomy, order and ardour. As a matter of history, Christians have from the first chosen one side or the other, quarrelsomely; and most Irish Christians, following a bent which is a good deal more marked in the Irish than the British character, have been strong for authority. The intellectual basis of sectarian division is extremely durable.

Reconciliation is far off

So reconciliation is already far off. The most that can be substituted for it is a respectful acknowledgment of invincible differences. Yet I find it increasingly hard to avoid the conclusion that even that acknowledgment is prevented by Britain's continued military and political presence.

90 Britain's continued military presence

The military presence, first, obscures Britain's genuinely altruistic intentions. There have been several recent reminders that an army makes a poor police force: its members are not recruited for their tact, its weaponry is disproportionate. Even a plastic bullet (a solid fawn-coloured cylinder the size of a small tin of soup) can crack a skull. The effort to liberate working people in each community from thrall to its own 100 strongarm men has only generated anger against the liberators.

Britain's continued political presence

More, the Army is a highly visible sign of Britain's dominant political presence. That presence stultifies local dialogue. Political leaders on both sides still demand, in the teeth of what is either right or practicable, that Britain shall make their side win.

Another arm of Britain's political presence is 110 the Treasury. Certain Government benefits hide the real cost of violence from its partisans. Active paramilitary men – members of the Provisional IRA or the Ulster Defence Association – can get their daily bread from the dole. The Provisionals can tell themselves that to destroy businesses and with them jobs – the Province's crying need – damages not the Northern Ireland worker but only the British Government, obliged as the civil power to pay compensation.

120 (It now pays out compensation at the rate of £250.000 a day, or £90 million a year. That is even more than the extra annual cost of the Army's operations, now approaching £80 million.)

(John Whale,
The Sunday Times, October 30, 1976)

What you have to do

Comment/Teamwork

Prepare a short speech in class on:

"Why reconciliation has failed in Ulster so far".

Refer to the following aspects in your speech:

Comment/Teamwork

1. Where can you see that reconciliation has failed so far in Ulster?
2. What role does the Catholic Church play in this context according to the author?
3. Whom does the author blame for the failure and how does he support his view?
4. Does the author convince you?

How the IRA gained a sniper

MARY HOLLAND interviews a wounded IRA gunman in hiding who admits to firing on a British soldier in Londonderry last Sunday.

LONDONDERRY, 5 February THERE was one IRA sniper wounded here last Sunday. He was a member of the ' official ' IRA, and he was posted in an empty house on the corner of Cooke Street and Joyce Street, with orders to cover Bishop Street.

He was wounded by a soldier returning fire from a house opposite after he himself had fired at a soldier in the street beneath. He thinks his bullet grazed the soldier's flak jacket, but did not injure him.

The Army may well think that they killed him. He was hit in the thigh by one bullet and another ricochetted off a wall to graze the flesh of his eye. By the kind of coincidence common here, the soldier who fired on him was posted on the roof of the sniper's sister-in-law's house, and she heard him reporting back to his commanding officer, ' I think we got him, sir, we saw him fall.'

I talked to the sniper several times this week, while he nursed his gunshot wounds in the bedroom of the new Northern Ireland Housing Trust house into which his family recently moved.

I've known this man since 1968. His background is fairly typical of the boys round here. He left school at 15 and got a job in a local factory. When it closed he went to England and worked on building sites. He talks about the parks in London and how much he liked them. He didn't smoke or drink then, but went dog racing two or three times a week and then on to the Hammersmith Palais or some other dance hall.

' At that time I couldn't be bothered with politics.' he told me. ' I remember being in England and talking to someone in a park and it was election day. I didn't know.'

In 1966, when he was 22, he came back to Derry, got a place in the Government factory scheme and another job in a factory. He was still doing this in October 1968, when the first civil rights march took place.

' I remember being shocked at what I thought was the viciousness of some of the placards on that march.' One he said read, ' " The Tories are vermin—Bevan". I hadn't heard of Bevan. To me, people who went on marches were nut cases, but I went because a friend of mine asked me. Then, well you know what happened when the police charged, I couldn't believe it.

' Some people round here hated the police, but I'd always respected them. I associated them with the British bobby and at that time I thought the myth of the British bobby. I just couldn't take in what was happening. I saw a policeman raise his baton to a young girl and I stood there paralysed in front of him. There must have been horror on my face because he lowered his baton and walked away.

' After that my faith in the police was shaken. I continued to go on the civil rights marches, and there was I, always on peaceful demonstrations and they were always kicking the tripes out of me. Then in January 1969, after Burntollet [when a civil rights march was ambushed by militant Protestants], they came down into the area at nights and terrorised the people in their homes. From that time on I was finished with the police.

' That was the first time I began to think that we ought to be able to defend ourselves I still haven't thought out the political implications of that. The friend who'd taken me on the first march was always on at me to go to Labour Party meetings. I did go once, but I just didn't like it ; they seemed so dogmatic, so sure of themselves.

' But after January 1969 and the riots. I went along to the Young Socialists, who were just starting up in Derry. They were far closer to me. For one thing, they were all ignorant like me, so we could learn together. ' I started to read trade union history. I became very worker conscious. I was obsessed with Protestant-Catholic unity.

' At that stage I thought we must not do anything to alienate the Protestant working class. Now I think that's hopeless at the moment, right out of the window. We can only make a new start here if we get rid of Stormont and all it represents.'

When did he first take up a gun ? ' After 1969, when the British Army came in. I knew we must never again be as defenceless as we had been against the RUC. I knew the soldiers had to come, that we weren't ready, couldn't handle the situation, but I knew too that they hadn't come here to protect us, they'd come to protect the *status quo.*

' When I heard the troops were coming and that Stormont was to stay. I knew it was defeat for us. I'd never held a gun at that time. I threw my first petrol bomb in those riots. Afterwards I was asked by the IRA if I wanted weapon training, and I said I did. I used to go along to classes here. Then last year the IRA in Dublin offered about 30 of us training in Donegal, with no strings attached, just in case we ever needed to defend this area, and I went along. But I still didn't join.

' Even after October 1968,' he said, ' the one group I never thought of joining was the Republican movement. To me, Republicans were tight, small men with narrow minds. Perhaps it was my background. We were never nationalist in this house.'

Internment changed that. It was announced on 9 August last year. 'On that morning I was working in Dublin. I was making good money selling ice-cream and I was really enjoying Dublin. I was involved with left-wing groups down South. I still hadn't joined the Republicans. I packed in my job and came home that day.

At first I busied myself with things like the radio transmitter and producing leaflets. but I knew in my mind I was just putting off facing up to the fact that it was going to mean shooting people. Someone said to me "that's what you'll be at when they come in to gun down our women and children. firing leaflets back at them." And I knew he was right—that I approved in principle of shooting soldiers and that it was moral cowardice on my part not to face doing it.

'So when the official IRA asked me to join I agreed. The first job I was sent to reconnoitre, I just walked up and down the street for two hours. I looked at the soldiers on duty and two of them were kids of about 17 and the one with a stripe about 21. I said to myself, "sure they're nothing but a couple of wains." I couldn't shoot them. It's different now. It's all different now.

'Up till last Sunday I didn't want to shoot soldiers. I'd do it if I was told to. but only because I was told to and believed it necessary. Now I'll go looking for them. I'll take every opportunity I can.'

The Observer, February 6, 1972

Work sheet: "How the IRA gained a sniper"

Questions on the text

Read all the question first and plan your answers carefully in order to avoid repeating yourself. Use your own words as far as possible.

1. Summarize in about 100 words the young man's development from October 1968 to January 30, 1972.
2. Characterize the young man's changing attitude towards the British army and explain his underlying motives!
3. What effect does Mary Holland want to achieve by the way she has worded the headline?
4. Try to determine the author's attitude toward the issue. Support your view by giving evidence from the text.
5. Paraphrase three of the following four passages from the text. Do not use the words in italics.
   – "To me, people who went on mar-
   – ches were *nut cases*" (line 68–69)
   – "I *thought the world* of the British bobby" (line 79–80)
   – "they were always *kicking the tripes out* of me" (line 94–95)
   – "I was *finished with* the police" (line 102–103)
6. Explain in what way these expressions are typical of the person interviewed in the article.
7. What does "Protestant-Catholic unity„ (line 125) mean in this text?
8. What does the young man mean with "Stormont and all it represents" (line 133)?
9. Do you think that the young man takes part in acts of terrorism against civilians in Northern Ireland? Give reasons for your answer!
10. What do you think is the young man's attitude toward civil rights marches or peace marches in Northern Ireland today?

Comment

Do you agree with the following three statements given by English people when asked what they thought of the British army's role on "Bloody Sunday"! Write a short comment of about 80 words.

Elderly lady in Lambeth: "It's not the Army's fault they're in Ireland. It doesn't matter whether they're doing a good job or not, they're only doing what they have to".

Her friend agreed: "If the Irish want to fight, let them fight among themselves. Why should our boys risk their lives? I can't worry about the Irish dead. It's their own fault".

Stockbroker:: "Bloody Sunday"? They asked for it and they got it".

The Observer, February 6, 1972

Composition

Choose one of the following subjects. Write about 150 words.

1. Write a letter to the editor, criticizing the publication of an interview with an IRA gunman.
2. Write a letter to the editor, approving of this article as important background information for understanding the complex situation in Northern Ireland.
3. "Demonstrations as means to achieve political aims". Write an introductory speech for a classroom debate on this issue. (You may put forward some provocative ideas in order to stimulate a lively discussion!)

Comprehension piece

Why the Army is there

From foreign comment on events in Northern Ireland it is evident that they are widely seen in terms of an orthodox colonial situation: a native population bravely struggling to free itself from a regime of foreign exploitation. The official publicity put around by the government of the Republic of Ireland favours that version, a version which bears no truthful relation to the reason for the British military presence in Northern Ireland, or the justification for it, or the conduct of it.

There are two communities in the north-east corner of Ireland, one predating the other. The second, derived chiefly from Scotland and partly from England, began to be established by right of conquest in the early years of the seventeenth century. Its length of tenure is therefore approximately equal to that of the communities descended from the English plantations in North America.

The two communities in north-east Ireland have not been assimilated. The original ground of animosity – the distrust and resentment that must exist between confiscator and dispossessed – was reinforced by Christian sectarianism. The descendants of the dispossessed adhered for the most part to the religion of Rome, while the descendants of the newcomers remained Presbyterians, other Dissenters, and members of the Established Church. At times the Roman Catholics and Dissenters were able to make common cause in protest against the civil and religious disabilities that both suffered. But these temporary alliances did not melt sectarian separatism, which became generalized into contrasting patterns of culture, loyalty, education, social institutions, and moral exemplars. The differences became tribal in character.

In the nineteenth century Ireland was an integral part of the United Kingdom. In Belfast there was chronic tension between Orangemen and Catholics, frequent riots, much bloodshed and a standing role for the soldiery. It was the inability of these two communities in Ireland to live within a common polity without fighting that led to partition of the country in 1921, twenty-six Irish counties being granted quasi-independence, since completed, and six remaining part of the United Kingdom and being given provincial institutions of subordinate self-government which they did not seek.

The assimilation of the two communities in north-east Ireland which three centuries without partition did not achieve was not achieved by fifty years of partition either. The ancestral animosities dozed for a bit but never departed. Everybody has his own explanation of why that is and points the finger at his chosen culprit. But it is the fact of those potentially murderous animosities, not the reason for them, that British policy has had to reckon with first of all.

The eruption of those animosities into communal violence caused the British Government to deploy the Army for the restoration of civil peace in August 1969. For that purpose it remains. But it has had forced on it a second, and at present more conspicuous, role.

Protestants stand to Roman Catholics in the province of Northern Ireland in the ratio of two to one. On the likely assumption that *in extremis* nearly all Catholics are sympathetic to a united and independent Ireland and that nearly all Protestants stand by the union with Great Britain, there is a heavy majority in favour of the union. Provincial elections have consistently confirmed that conclusion.

Nevertheless a faction of the Irish Republican Army embarked on a campaign of violent insurrection with the avowed purpose of incorporating the province of Northern Ireland in an all-Ireland republic, to erase by force the settled resolution of the majority. The second role of the Army is to meet and defeat that conspiracy of violence.

In that conflict non-belligerents, including women and children, are at risk. Most of the killing, maiming and destruction of property is the work of the IRA. Sometimes the innocent suffer at the hands of the Army, too. That is deeply regrettable but it is not wholly avoidable so long as the challenge of violent insurrection against the majority is sustained.

In the Republic of Ireland opinion has worked itself up into the furious belief that the British Army are acting as wanton oppressors. The intensity of belief – even the burning of an embassy – does not make it true. The Army is there primarily to prevent communal carnage, secondly to defeat an armed attack upon the state by a minority of a minority, and thirdly to hold the ring while statesmen make a further attempt to find a political framework that will accommodate in peace the two historic communities in the north of Ireland.

Foreign governments should be extremely cautious of proceeding on any other assumption, and particularly on the crude distortion that the role of the British Government and Army in Northern Ireland is that of a colonial oppressor. The Irish themselves will not be served by that misconception. There is real danger of civil war which would spread throughout the island. It is held back by the presence and operations of the British Army.

The Times, February 3, 1972

Work sheet: "Why The Army Is There"

Questions on the text

Read all the questions first and plan your answers carefully in order to avoid repeating yourself. Use your own words as far as possible.

1. How has the author arranged his text?
   Divide the text into four paragraphs and give a heading to each!

2. What reasons does the author give for Britain's presence in Ireland from the early 17th century up to 1921 and how does he justify this presence during that period?

3. What does the author want to show by comparing the north-east of Ireland with North America?

4. In line 44–49 the author implicitly refers to the United Irishmen's Rebellion in 1798. Why doesn't he mention who the rebels made a common cause against and what they aimed at?

5. Why doesn't the author continue referring to the American example?

6. Comment on the author's view of the partition of Ireland!

7. Is the author justified to be rather short on
   – the 19th century in Anglo-Irish history
   – the late 1960s in Northern Ireland?
   Answer either part a) or part b) of this question!

8. What are the reasons and the justification for the British military presence in Ireland according to the text?
9. Compare the first and the last paragraph of the leading article:
In what way does the author react differently to the attack from abroad that Britain is a colonial power in Northern Ireland?

What is the twofold message of the last paragraph?
10. Does the author "point the finger at his chosen culprit"? Look up his account of the period between the early 17th century and 1969 first and then the period after 1969!

Comment on the language

Answer *one* of the following questions:

1. The author uses quite a number of different expressions for the two communities in Ireland/Northern Ireland in the course of his arguments:

one community predating the other	– the other derived chiefly from Scotland and partly from England
dispossessed descendants of the dispossessed	– confiscator
	– descendants of the newcomers
Roman Catholics	– Dissidents
Catholics	– Orangemen
Roman Catholics	– Protestants
Catholics	– Protestants
minority	– heavy majority

Which impression is the reader left with about the nature of the conflict in Northern Ireland?

2. Covering Anglo-Irish history up to 1969 the author uses the expression "animosities" (between the two communities) or synonymous expressions twelve times. Covering the situation after 1969 the author refers only once to animosities ("communal carnage") between the two communities.
What impression is the reader left with about the nature of the conflict in Northern Ireland?

Composition

1. The author puts down his attitude towards the conflict in Northern Ireland in the sentence "But it is the fact of those potentially murderous animosities, not the reason for them, that British policy has had to reckon with first of all".
How would he express this attitude in a personal statement in colloquial language? (Write about 80 words!)
2. Write a letter to the editor (about 150 words) referring to the TIMES leader.

Write your letter from the point of view of **one** of the following persons:
– an Englishman
– a Catholic from Northern Ireland
– a Protestant from Northern Ireland
– an Eire Government official
– an American of Irish origin, whose great-grandfather emigrated to America during the Great Famine in the 184Os

Translation

Translate into German the first two paragraphs of a letter to the editor, published in the Times, 5 February 1972.

Text

The Times, 5 February 1972
Letters to the editor
From Mr M. B. Irvine, Cambridge

Sir,

In your leader of February 3 you give what most people will agree is an accurate and succinct account of the origin of the two communities in Ulster. You go on to argue that the unrest there is not the result of an "orthodox colonial situation: a native population bravely struggling to free itself from a regime of foreign exploitation", and you castigate the government of the Republic of Ire-
10 *land for tendentious misrepresentation. With respect, Sir, I submit that you are mistaken; it is fundamentally a colonial situation if not an entirely orthodox one (whatever the meaning of this word may be in this context).*

May I first take up your comparison of the Ulster Unionist community with that of the North American continent, deriving from the New England settlement. It is true that their tenure of the soil of their respective countries is roughly of
20 *equal duration, but there has been a vital difference in their psychological development, in that in the eighteenth century the American colonists broke the umbilical cord uniting them to the English motherland and affirmed themselves as an independent community.* (184 words)

Part 4:
Solutions

What can be done?

British statesmen have not been prepared to devote to Ireland the amount of time and attention its good government required. They have attempted, in all Ireland in the more distant past and in Northern Ireland in the recent past, to rule Ireland through a colony. This has failed. "Planters and natives" can undoubtedly come to an agreement in Ireland, perhaps an agreement to continue in some form the partition of the country, but it seems to me essential that those who are responsible for government in Ireland should be rooted in the country and committed to it – and ultimately dependent on Irish resource and initiatives to solve Ireland's problems. What keeps the sterile quarrel of Orange and Green alive is the constant presence of the third party, Great Britain.

Liam de Paor, Divided Ulster, p. xix

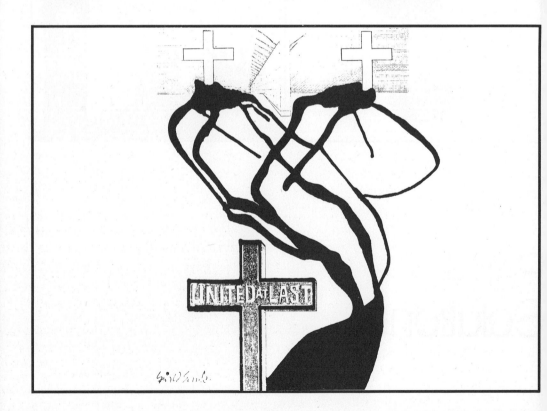

ULSTER, BLOODY ULSTER

Should we get out?

AFTER the horror of the latest— and worst — Ulster massacre, the demand from the rest of Britain will become irresistible: **LET ULSTER STEW IN HER OWN BLOODY JUICE.**

And can you blame them ?

For the British Government cannot indefinitely take responsibility for a country in which "law and order" is a sick joke.

The Army cannot indefinitely take responsibility for a situation which it cannot control. . A situation which no army could control, except maybe the Nazi SS.

Northern Ireland Secretary Merlyn Rees, the man with the impossible job, says:

"Something has got to emerge" in the Ulster community to stop the killing "because extra soldiers, extra police by themselves just will not do it."

Is this the best the Government can offer?

The hope that something will turn up. The hope that somehow things will get better. That the terrorists will go away.

The truth is there is no real policy for Ulster. No high level political debate. No sign of fresh thinking from Mr. Wilson.

Successive British Governments have tried every way they could to impose sweet reason on

MIRROR COMMENT

the unreasoning Ulster factions.

There was the Sunningdale agreement by which the Protestant lion would lie down in peace with the Catholic tiger.

There was the Ulster convention in which the two sides would hopefully agree to grasp hands and share power.

Where are those hopes now ? **Smashed** by the Ulster workers' strike. **Wrecked** by IRA murders and Protestant murders. **Swept away** in a hail of bullets as Catholics are gunned down in their homes and Protestants are lined up and shot.

Britain has withdrawn from other countries. Sometimes, as in India, withdrawal has been followed by slaughter on an appalling scale.

The withdrawal was made because there was no other choice.

Is there any other choice for Britain in Ulster ? As things are shaping the answer must be **NO**.

Let the IRA and their supporters be very clear on one point.

Britain cannot and must not walk out of Ulster leaving no authority behind. Britain must hand over power

to some properly constituted Government.

AND THAT GOVERNMENT WILL INEVITABLY BE A PROTESTANT GOVERNMENT.

That is a fact of arithmetic in an independent Ulster. The Protestants are the majority.

It would be a very tough Government indeed.

Is this what the IRA want? Is this what the Catholic community wants? Is this what Eire wants?

Nobody wants the tortured people of Ulster to be tortured even more cruelly. No British Government wants blood on its conscience.

From: Daily Mirror, January 7, 1976

Notes on the text:

bloody: lit. = full of blood, sl. = damned

the latest and worst Ulster massacre: in the worst sectarian incident in terms of deaths in Northern Ireland since 1969 10 Protestant workers were massacred in a mini-bus in a machine-gun attack in Northern Ireland's troubled co. Armagh on 5. January 1976. The massacre was believed to be an IRA reprisal for the killing of five Catholics in the same area of Ulster the day before.

let sb. stew in his own juice: idiom. be left without help to take the consequences of one's actions.

unreasoning Ulster factions: the different political groups involved who refuse to solve things reasonably.

Sunningdale: London-Dublin-Belfast conference on 6.−9. 12. 1973 which agreed on establishing a Council of Ireland. The agreement was never put into practice.

Ulster Convention: 1 May 1974. Election in Northern Ireland to a Constitutional Convention which was to draw up a new constitution for Northern Ireland on the basis of some form of power-sharing and partnership between the Catholic and Protestant communities. It was dissolved on 5 March 1976 by the British Government without any further progress having been made.

Ulster workers' strike: strike by militant Protestant workers on 15 May 1974 which paralysed Ulster.

What you have to do

Guided Analysis

Guided Analysis

Answer the following questions:

1. How many paragraphs can you distinguish in the author's line of argument? Give short headings!
2. How does the author's attitude towards the Irish troubles change within the comment?
3. Characterize the author's attitude in the first column towards the people in Britain, the British Government, the British Army and the Northern Ireland Secretary!
4. What conclusions does the author draw from six years of British policy in Northern Ireland?
5. Who does he blame for the failure?
6. Why does he give the example of India?
7. How does he answer the question asked in the headline?
8. What will "inevitably" be the consequence of the solution proposed by the author?
9. Why doesn't the author write it *will be* "a very tough Government indeed"?
10. What is the effect of the three questions at the end of the comment?
11. In what way does the lay-out of the text support the author's arguments?

'Civil war if we quit Ulster'

In an important intervention in the Ulster independence debate, Airey Neave, a Conservative frontbencher, yesterday sounded "a note of warning." He said in Cardiff that independence would make it more difficult for Northern Ireland to live in peace

❛ Let us examine the arguments. First, there is the argument that the "British presence" is the divisive element in Northern Ireland. This is an extraordinary distortion. Northern Ireland is part of the United Kingdom at the expressed wish of the overwhelming majority of its citizens and not because of British imperial ambitions. We are not dealing with a colonial situation — as Dublin ministers themselves have on several occasions pointed out. The partition of Ireland is the result of disagreements between Irishmen, and not of a British determination to keep a foothold in the island.

British troops became involved in the Northern Ireland crisis in 1969 in what appeared to be a civil war which the Royal Ulster Constabulary was unable to control. What possible evidence can there be that, if those troops were removed now, commonsense, peace and harmony would reign? It is a dangerous and perhaps suicidal illusion.

Powerful para-military organisations exist today on both sides of Northern Ireland, anxious and willing to "have a go" at each other. It is not surprising that some of them should espouse the idea of an independent Ulster, since the situation which would follow a withdrawal of troops is the only one in which they could hope to gain power. If—as Fianna Fail politicians have suggested—Britain set a date for withdrawal a certain number of years ahead, it is reasonable to expect such people to begin to arm and organise themselves in advance. The ground would be cut from under the feet of all those working for peace and reconciliation.

Britain could not guarantee any settlement without the presence of troops. If we retained the right to intervene again should civil war break out, we would impose on ourselves the need to become involved in a far more difficult situation than at present. All available evidence suggests that a civil war of massive proportions would occur, and we would suffer the international opprobrium of having performed a Congo-type scuttle.

Ulster cannot have stable self-government other than by institutions widely accepted throughout the community. In what way would removal of the British facilitate that consent? There are many people in Ulster unwilling or unable to make any concessions today. Would promises to make them tomorrow in an independent Ulster bear fruit?

The IRA have made it clear that they will not accept an independent Northern Ireland. An independent Ulster would therefore have to meet and defeat a terrorist campaign with diminished financial and military resources.

There is a defeatist argument sometimes deployed in favour of withdrawal which says that seven years of violence have shown that the security forces cannot defeat the IRA and we should therefore leave the situation to find its own level.

I reject this argument for several reasons. I believe that a consistent and determined security campaign carried out within a stable constitutional framework could defeat the IRA. I am not prepared to accept that the British Army, after so many sacrifices in Northern Ireland, should bow to an enemy it has shown the capacity to defeat.

This would be a national humiliation. It would have wide implications for army morale and withdrawal would be the green light for other terrorist organisations throughout the world.

Our obligations in Ulster are not only those of duty—though they are certainly that—they are also those of self-interest. If a bloody civil war broke out in Ireland it would be naive to assume that it would not affect cities on this side of the Irish Sea.

Is it really credible that a Lebanon-type situation a few miles across the Irish Sea would not have immense repercussions on our society? And can we really be confident that whatever government emerged would be sympathetic to the Nato alliance?

An independent Northern Ireland would, on present figures, have to cut its public expenditure by a third or increase its taxation by half unless financial assistance continued from Britain. The assumption by certain advocates of independence that Britain could or would continue to pay out £500 million a year for 15 years to an independent Ulster should not be relied upon.

The Conservative Party are the party of the Union. We shall defend a Union based on shared purposes and loyalties and not on force. If it was clearly the overwhelming and agreed wish of the people of Northern Ireland that they should secede from the United Kingdom, then the decision would be theirs, though we would regret it. But there is not yet the slightest evidence that any significant body of electoral opinion in Northern Ireland supports this proposal ❜

The Sunday Times, November 21, 1976

Notes on the text:

to espouse: to give support to an idea

Fianna Fail: biggest political party in the Republic of Ireland. When founded in 1926, mildly radical and Republican, today conservative. In the EC it aligns itself with the French Gaullist party.

opprobium: public shame attaching to some act or conduct

Congo-type scuttle: the hurried departure of Belgium from its former colony

to deploy an argument: to put forward

public expenditure: money spent by the state

What you have to do

Version

Translate the following passage into German:
"Let us examine . . . suicidal illusion"

Guided analysis

Answer the following questions:

1. Divide the speech into paragraphs and find headings for each!
2. How does Mr Neave justify the "British presence" in Ulster?
3. Do you agree with Mr Neave's argument that partition is the result of disagreement between Irishmen?
4. What would be the result, according to Mr Neave, of a withdrawal from Northern Ireland?
5. What would be the difficulty for Britain if, after a withdrawal, she retained the right to intervene?
6. – Which example against a withdrawal is used by Mr Neave?
   – What does it prove?
   – How far is it counter-productive?
7. How would the IRA react towards an independent Ulster according to Mr Neave?
8. – What does Mr Neave mean by "defeatist argument"?
   – Do you agree with his arguments?
9. What would be the result of a British withdrawal from Ulster, in Mr Neave's opinion, on a national and international level?
10. What does Mr Neave mean with "duty" and "self-interest" as Britain's motives to stay in Ulster?
11. What does Mr Neave offer as a solution to the Ulster conflict?
12. Mr Neave poses quite a number of questions. Why doesn't he answer them?
13. – Who do you think this speech was addressed to?
    – How do you think the audience responded to this speech?

Writing a news article

Imagine yourself to be a journalist reporting on Airey Neave's speech in Cardiff.

Write a short news article with headline (about 100 words) either for the Daily Mirror or The Times.

Keep the readers of your paper in mind!

Joining the discussion after the speech
(Teamwork)

Prepare short statements for a discussion on Airey Neave's speech:
1. supporting his views fully
2. asking the Conservative frontbencher to be more specific on certain points
3. disagreeing with his views
4. taking a more moderate stand on the issue

One team should take Mr Neave's part in the discussion. This discussion may be held right after the analysis of the speech or at the end of this unit.

Why we should leave Ulster

by John Whale

We are as lost as we have always been. We have mismanaged our dealings with the island of Ireland for 800 years; and although our motive has changed in the past decade from self-interest to disinterest, the world does not perceive it, and neither do most of the Irish. It is an island where we are fated to be misunderstood as much as we misunderstand.

What, Then can be done?

The answer—the only answer we have not tried—is to pull the thorn out of the wound. The Government should announce a dated withdrawal. By a specified date in the future, the whole apparatus of British military and civilian power in Northern Ireland would be shipped back to the mainland. Northern Ireland itself would become independent.

Of all the questions which come crowding in, the most difficult concerns the length of the deadline.

The right interval between declaration and fulfilment would probably be not less than three years and not more than twelve.

The case against a dated withdrawal

The case against these proposals is at least fivefold:
1. Britain would be giving in to violence;
2. We would be leaving Northern Ireland's ports open to Russian submarines;
3. We would be abandoning our duty to govern;
4. We would be defaulting on pledges given to the Northern Ireland majority;
5. Certain Protestants would rise in wrath.

The case for a dated withdrawal

1. No violent men would be achieving their demands. The Protestant paramilitaries have no recognisable political programme. The Provisionals' main aim is for a 32-county socialist republic, which—given attitudes in the Republic—would still be as distant as the farthest star. They also want the Army to go home, true; but a good idea is not made bad because it is espoused by unscrupulous people.

2. This flag has been fetched out of the locker and run up again by John Biggs-Davison, the Conservative MP. But instead of barricading Belfast Lough, Britain would do more to discomfit the Russians by taking its highly trained soldiers off police work and restoring them to full-time service with our NATO forces on the continent of Europe.

101

3. Duty implies capacity. We have lost it.

4. Our pledges were given for the best, and would be withdrawn for the best. The cruel world has moved on. The sad figures are the Ulstermen who feel British and love Britain. Although they are not thick on the ground, they do exist, and deserve cherishing. But they can take comfort from the example of like-minded people in the South, who have ready access to British-owned shops, English books and broadcasting and newspapers, Scotch whisky, and the British mainland itself. None of that will be different in the North, after independence. Britain and Northern Ireland will stay friends. This is the only way they will.

5. Since there will be no immediate change, angry Protestants would have no occasion to rise in wrath. They might attempt a general strike on the 1974 model. But even if they were not defeated by their own discomfort, and won a British retraction, it would not be one they could trust. The withdrawal declaration will make actual what in their hearts they already know. The British have after all been openly trying to get clear of Ireland for 90 years—since Gladstone's first Home Rule Bill of 1886: and one day they will manage it.

An outcome with no losers

Many Protestants will welcome the declaration. Independence already has many backers, and will accumulate more as the melancholy logic of devolution pushes Scotland further and further that way. It constitutes the one feasible future left for Northern Ireland. It is the only outcome in which no one loses, and hence the only one which will stop the fighting.

The new administration would give the Catholic minority its part in power. Devising a method would not be as difficult as it has been. In a few years' time localised partition will have become the rule. Most people will have chosen to live in wholly Protestant or wholly Catholic enclaves. These could become new municipalities. West Belfast is an apt case.

The essence of a solution now is sorrowfully to accept the divisions and make them tidy.

The declaration would encourage a new realism and a new hope. Sectarian feeling would persist; but something of the bitterness would have gone out of it, because each sect would no longer be identified with a conflicting nationalism.

The Sunday Times,
October 31, 1976

Notes on the text:

deadline: fixed limit of time, e. g. before which sth. must be done

to default on pledges: to break given promises

not be thick on the ground: there are not many of them

they deserve cherising: they are worth caring for

in wrath: full of anger and hatred

retraction: taking back a plan

devolution: process of decentralization in Britain (dt. Autonomisierung, Föderalisierung)

feasible: realistic, sth. that can be managed

municipalities: parts of a city with self-government

What you have to do

Version
Guided analysis
Guided comment

Version

Translate the following passage into German:
"Many Protestants ... conflicting nationalism"

Guided analysis

Answer the following questions:

1. How does John Whale structure his line of argument?
2. What does he propose as a remedy for the Irish troubles?
3. What is his view of the defeatist argument?
4. Does he think the strategic argument to be still relevant?
5. What is his opinion of Britain's obligation to stay in Ulster?
6. Does he think that Britain is defaulting her pledges given to the majority in Northern Ireland?
7. Why is he optimistic about the Protestant reaction to a British withdrawal?
8. Do you agree with John Whale that a dated withdrawal will provide an outcome with no losers?
9. Explain the last sentence of the text within the context of 800 years of Anglo-Irish history!

Guided Comment

"Three views on a British withdrawal from Northern Ireland".
Use the following questions as a guide line for your comment:

Questions:

1. Which view strikes you as one-sided?
2. Which view suggests the most radical solution?
3. Whose solution is based on an analysis of the conflict?
4. Who appeals mostly to feelings particularly of fear?
5. What rhetorical devices are used and to what effect?
6. Which of the authors, in your opinion, has learnt most from Britain's history as a colonial power?

Extra material

Text 1 *The Sunday Times, November 7, 1976*

In a leader page article on October 31, John Whale advocated a dated withdrawal of Britain's military and political presence from Northern Ireland, followed by independence.

Sir,
A few thousand killed over a five-year period can hardly be described as unbearable. I, and most of the people I talk to, seem to take a certain pride in watching our lads on TV charging around chasing one sort of rioter or another.
Yours faithfully
N. J. Mustoe
Tarpoley

Text 2 *The Sunday Times, November 14, 1976*

Dangers of an Ulster pull-out

In reply, **The Rt Hon Harry West,** Leader of the Ulster Unionist Party and of the United Ulster Unionist Party, argues that there is not in any politically effective sense "two communities." Indeed, there is a strong shared sense of identity among Ulster people. Nor, says Mr West, does political alignment correspond with differences of religious affiliation. He continues:

The main source of sectarian bitterness has been the fact that Republican activists have tried, in the past as well as recently, to achieve a take-over of the Roman Catholic part of our community. For what Mr Whale calls reconciliation there is in Ulster a very general desire; but it can become socially and politically effective only when Republican terrorism is decisively defeated. If this is only to be "contained" and kept at "an acceptable level" the urge for reconciliation will not achieve the fulfilment we wish for it. Meanwhile some of the schemes by which the British Government has tried to reconcile the supposed "two communities" have been sharply divisive in effect, creating new forms of self-conscious difference.

In the Constitutional Convention last year we produced a plan for future community government which committed most public business to departmental parliamentary committees on which elected representatives from government and opposition would sit in equal numbers. We were told by specialists that this represented the most advanced scheme for democratic community participation in government in the modern world.

In an atmosphere of extending consensus, this won the support of two-thirds of the members of the Convention; and others clearly approved of many of its principles. At this point, however, the Government rejected our plan out of hand and closed the Convention, together with the machinery it had provided for inter-party negotiations. Her Majesty's Government was thus unwilling to allow politics in Northern Ireland to find its own level.

Northern Ireland has had four general elections in two years, in which the clearly expressed aspirations of the electorate have each time been denied any practical implementation. It has been ruled for over four-and-a-half years by an expensive and ineffective bureaucratic dictatorship. There is no spirit of reconciliation in this. Often we have been told that we ought to prefer the ballot to the bullet and that is how nearly all of us want to have it.

But a growing body of Ulster opinion has unhappily become convinced that the Government prefers the bullet and that it is in its heart opposed to peace and reconciliation in any politically realistic form. Hence our present deadlocked and deteriorating situation has caused 1,600 deaths —an equivalent of 62,000 if proportionately applied to the population of Britain.

When so much has been pulled down and so little permitted to be built, a British pull-out would create a dangerous vacuum and a most serious threat to the free world. The British presence in Ulster could be helpful and creative for the future. It cannot, however, achieve this while it is shut off from reality by untrue mental image and is not prepared to respond to the aspirations of Ulster people or the practical co-operation it can receive from them.

The following two letters refer to an editorial article in The Observer, 20 October 1974 by Kevin O'Neill: "Time for a radical solution in Ulster". O'Neill, a former lecturer at University College, Dublin, now working in Paris, outlined a bold plan for an eventual solution of the problems of the province. He wrote: ". . . British rule must go, once and for all, and the Irish — all the Irish — must be left to solve their own problems . . . What is essential is that Ulster should achieve independence — or have independence thrust upon it".

Text 3 *The Observer, 27 October 1974*

To the Editor of
The Observer
    Your editorial "Time for a Radical Solution in Ulster" last Sunday is not only an enlightened one, but very encouraging also. As you state, a British withdrawal at a fixed time is the very necessary first step to an Ulster solution.
    Experience tells us, and history will prove, that it is Britain's misfortune to withdraw too late and too slowly from places in which it should never have been in the first instance. I do not for a moment suggest that peace in Ulster will follow automatically once British troops withdraw. But such a withdrawal will surely be a basis upon which the people of Ulster can begin to build some structure for co-existence.

Father Cyril Haran
(Editor, The Angelus)
Sligo

Text 4 *The Observer, 27 October 1974*

    Kevin O'Neill's argument is entirely unconvincing. His case rests upon the quite unwarranted thesis that British presence is the major problem preventing more settled conditions prevailing between Catholics and Protestants. This argument also advanced by both wings of the IRA — is simply not supported by the facts. Britain is not standing in the way of a peaceful settlement to the Northern Ireland crisis. Happily, despite their differences, both communities in Northern Ireland are only too well aware that the British "presence" (a feature it should be realised, desired by an overwhelming majority of all the people in Northern Ireland) is presently the major factor preventing total bloody civil war — a civil war which would not be confined to the six counties of Northern Ireland.

Brian Garrett
(Chairman, Northern Ireland Labour Party)
Belfast

On 3 February 1972, a few days after "Bloody Sunday" The Times published a leading article "Why the Army is there". One of the following two letters to the editor of The Times was published on 31 January 1972, the other on 4 February 1972, referring to the leader as well as the letter published before.

Text 5 *The Times, February 3, 1972*

Sir,
    The time has come to say No. We must not permit the desperate and seemingly inexorable slide into massacre and brutality in Northern Ireland to continue towards its only-too-logical culmination.
    The historical parallels for the situation today in Ireland are clear and painful; we have been through it all before in almost everyone of the individual episodes of Britain's long-drawn-out retreat from Empire. Even more clearly there stands before us the spectre of the French experience in Algeria and the American example in Vietnam. The sequence which runs through the involvement of troops in support of an oppressive civil power, the resulting popular protest, and the cycle of arrests and shootings, protests and further arrests, torture, brutality and the systematic degradation of the oppressed popula-tion by legal, semi-legal and straightforwardly totalitarian tactics, has consequences which are profound for the oppressors as well as the oppressed. A sort of moral gangrene sets in, only too plain in France over Algeria, and in the USA as a consequence of Vietnam today.
    A home population becomes increasingly callous and indifferent to reports of the behaviour of troops acting in their name. But the consequences of indifference soon become felt at home as well. Must we wait before troops blooded in Derry are turned against strikers or the unemployed closer at hand? For those who feel such a possibility far-fetched, let it be recalled that it is barely three years ago that the then Home Secretary categorically assured the nation that CS gas would not be used in the dispersion and control of demonstrators. Both the scale and

technology of the military actions have moved
far since then. To remain silent or indifferent
40 under these circumstances would be an unforgive-
able intellectual and social treason.

We write as individuals to appeal to all those
who feel the necessity to make collective public
demand for an end to the involvement of British
troops in Northern Ireland, an end to internment
and end to its associated brutality, an end to the

use of legal and administrative devices as instrument of collective punishment of the Catholic
population.

50 Yours faithfully,

Stephen Rose,
Peter Townsend
108 Regent's Park Rd.
London NW 1
31/1/1972

Text 6 *The Times, February 4, 1972*

Sir,

Even with a generous allowance for their
expected Pavlovian reactions, the letter from Prof.
Rose and Mr. Peter Townsend (Febr. 4) is a little
hard to swallow.

They tell us that the Ulster crisis is part of
"Britain's long-drawn-out retreat from Empire",
with an "oppressed population" in arm against
the brutal British. They are presumably aware
10 that Ulster is not a colony but part of the United
Kingdom, and that rather more than two-thirds
of the population of Ulster want the British troops
to stay in order to prevent the majority from being
murdered or handed over to the rule of what is
to most of them an alien country.

But let us, for the moment, grant them their
totally false historical analogy. Wherever the
British imperial power has been withdrawn from
a part of its empire, there has always been insist-
20 ence upon granting independence only in conditions of majority rule – except in Southern Africa.
Hinc illae lacrimae. Your correspondents can
only deny to the Ulster Protestants what they
demand for the Africans in Rhodesia by denying
that Northern Ireland exists at all.

In other words, they want the Ulster majority
to be forcibly transformed into an Irish minority.
I do not know by what historical warrant they
allege the unity of an Ireland that has never been
30 formally or informally united except artificially
and by force under British rule.

What is certain is that two-thirds of the population of Ulster denies this unity and will fight to
prevent it. Nothing would more certainly preci-
pitate the civil war than the removal of the British
troops now. It would be perhaps a salutary experience for Prof. Rose and Mr. Townsend to
travel the length of Ulster and ask the Protestants
majority for their views. But I suppose little can
40 be expected of men who pen down a violent
diatribe against those who seek to maintain law
and order within the United Kingdom, without a
word of censure or regret for the indiscriminate
murder of IRA bombings.

Is it their view that the gunman is always right –
even when his aim is the forcible destruction of
the rights of a peaceful majority?

Yours faithfully,

Angus Maude
House of Commons
4/2/1972

What
you have
to do

Write a letter to the editor!

1. Read these letters to the editor carefully. The arguments are already
   familiar to you. Therefore concentrate
   on the way the correspondents
   present their arguments in their letters.
2. Now write your letter to the editor
   referring *either* to one of the three
   articles on the issue *or* to one of the
   letters printed above. Keep in mind:
   "The best letter is a short letter".

The key results

Six options for Northern Ireland

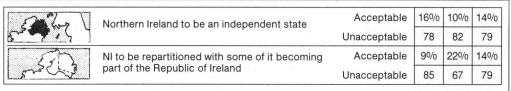

Which of these suggestions for solving the problem in Northern Ireland is acceptable?

		PROTESTANTS	CATHOLICS	ALL
Northern Ireland to be an independent state	Acceptable	16%	10%	14%
	Unacceptable	78	82	79
NI to be repartitioned with some of it becoming part of the Republic of Ireland	Acceptable	9%	22%	14%
	Unacceptable	85	67	79

● Two options – repartition and an independent Northern Ireland – are overwhelmingly rejected by the vast majority of voters, both Protestant and Catholic.

		PROTESTANTS	CATHOLICS	ALL
NI to be a part of a federal Irish state but with its own assembly with guarantees for Protestants	Acceptable	13%	58%	30%
	Unacceptable	80	31	62
NI to be fully integrated with the Republic of Ireland	Acceptable	6%	58%	25%
	Unacceptable	91	33	70

● Two other solutions – a federal Irish state with guarantees for Ulster Protestants; and a united Ireland – are acceptable to a majority of Catholics (though one in t h r e e Catholics *opposes* a united Ireland). But they are completely unacceptable to the majority of Protestants.

		PROTESTANTS	CATHOLICS	ALL
Northern Ireland to be fully integrated with the United Kingdom	Acceptable	91%	39%	72%
	Unacceptable	6	51	23

● One solution, permanent integration with the United Kingdom, has overwhelming Protestant support, but is rejected by over half the Catholics.

POWER SHARING

		PROTESTANTS	CATHOLICS	ALL
NI to remain part of the UK but with its own assembly with guarantees for Catholics	Acceptable	70%	62%	67%
	Unacceptable	23	32	26

● The remaining "power-sharing" option – that Northern Ireland should stay part of the UK, but with its own assembly and with guarantees for the Catholic minority – turns out to be acceptable to two people in three. Though somewhat more popular with Protestants than Catholics, it commands the support of 62 per cent of Catholic voters too.

As a solution it has the immense merit that it offends most people least.

THE ARMY

Which of these statements best describes your attitude to the British Army's future in Northern Ireland?	PROTESTANTS	CATHOLICS	ALL
The British Army should stay in Northern Ireland at its present numerical strength	57%	30%	47%
The British Army should stay at an increased numerical strength	26	3	17
The British Army should stay at a reduced numerical strength	10	20	14
The British Army should be withdrawn from Northern Ireland	6	41	19

It has been suggested that the British government could encourage a political settlement by announcing a date for withdrawing the army. Do you agree?		PROTESTANTS	CATHOLICS	ALL
	Agree	7%	49%	22%
	Disagree	87	34	68
	Dont't know/neither	5	17	10

There has been a remarkable collapse in Catholic support for the British Army's presence in Northern Ireland. In 1976, only 17 per cent of Catholics wanted the British army withdrawn; and a further 7 per cent wanted its strength reduced. Today, however, 41 per cent want the troops out; and a further 17 per cent want their numbers reduced.

Most dramatically of all, half of all Catholics say that Britain could encourage a political settlement by announcing a date for withdrawing the army.

When the army arrived in the province, it was seen by most Catholics as a guarantee of their safety. It is no longer so. With this, its chances of winning the support of the Catholic community in the fight against terrorism is immeasurably reduced.

THE SCHOOLS

Do you think Catholic and Protestant children should go to the same schools?		PROTESTANTS	CATHOLICS	ALL
	Yes	75%	66%	72%
	No	16%	25%	19%

MORI conducted the interviews with a representative quota sample of 1,008 respondents aged 18+ in 72 sampling points in Northern Ireland. The sample was designed to reflect the sex, age, social class and religious composition of the population of Northern Ireland as a whole. The fieldwork was carried out between June 18 and 22, 1981.

(The Sunday Times, June 28, 1981)

But there isn't any easy solution

Over the past two weeks The Sunday Times has interviewed many people in Northern Ireland, representing every strand of opinion in this tortured province.

What the voter actually wants to happen

Our poll shows that the majority of people favour a form of power-sharing – that much-abused but never properly tested system which would give both the half-million Catholics and the million Protestants a say in governing their own province.

Our poll suggested that, like most people in the United Kingdom, the people of Northern Ireland would like a political system run by men of moderate and reasonable views. The trouble is that, when it comes to entering the polling booth, traditional loyalties usually dictate a return to traditional parties. And these, far from offering the moderate option, tend to define their positions with narrow rigidity.

It is arguable, therefore, that the main political parties in Northern Ireland are standing in the way of what the voter actually wants to happen.

So what are the chances of these aspirations being translated into action? Our next task was to determine whether the politicians were prepared to contemplate the idea of a new power-sharing system. Here we plunged, inevitably, into the harsh reality of Northern Ireland politics.

What Protestant politicians fear

"There will never, never, ever be a united Ireland," says Robinson, MP and deputy leader of Ian Paisley's party.

"It's like saying Spain should take over Portugal. Have you seen the kind of people they are asking us to join?"

Such extreme reactions are fuelled by the belief that Britain is looking for a way out of Ireland. Ever since Gladstone, the history of Ireland has been one of Britain giving ground slowly but surely. So the Ulster Protestants have never felt totally secure. "We see ourselves as British, but when we go to England they don't see us as British," complains one local newspaper editor. Since Mrs Thatcher's historic visit to Dublin in December 1980 they have felt more insecure than ever.

Does she ever go anywhere to 'LISTEN'?

MAGGIE IN IRELAND TO TALK = Π = Calman

(The Times, Dec. 9, 1980)

Most Protestants we talked to are determined to resist any break with Britain – with force if necessary. However, we also found a small but growing number of Protestants who seemed resigned to some kind of union with the South.

The emotional favourite of the Protestants is Stormont

The emotional favourite of the Protestants is still a parliament at Stormont. It stands for 50 years of Protestant security and ascendancy. They believe their real troubles began when Stormont was disbanded in 1972 and they want it back.

Stormont, they feel, gives them some kind of protection. This is one reason why some Protestants would accept imposed power-sharing or partnership: it would at least give them Stormont back. But is it too late?

What the moderate SDLP wants

Power-sharing is no longer enough for the moderate Catholic SDLP. This is one of the key points emerging from our interviews. After the SDLP tasted power sharing in 1974 it said it would never accept anything less. Now, having seen Mrs Thatcher discussing Anglo-Irish relations with the Irish Prime Minister, it is unwilling to accept anything less than a settlement within this Irish dimension.

This is the scenario the SDLP now favours. First persuade the British government to end its guarantee of the Protestant position – "otherwise the Protestants won't negotiate anything. Then bide time while the Unionists "shout and moan" and eventually demand independence.

The SDLP would then welcome this demand because it would require negotiations about how to fund the new state. From these negotiations, the SDLP hopes, would come a federal solution with a parliament in the North and British citizenship for those who wished to retain it.

Unlikely solutions

Other options, however, are far less plausible. For instance, getting Britain to announce it will withdraw and leave the Irish to work out their own solution is considered seriously only by the IRA. And one Catholic politician told us: "Their problem is that they are cut off from talking to anyone but themselves. They don't have a chance to test their ideas against reality."

An equally unlikely solution is repartition – redrawing the boundary to produce a smaller, more Protestant Northern Ireland. This was dismissed as "demented" by one Catholic politician because it would back the Protestants into a highly vulnerable corner.

Overall, the main message from our interviews in the North was that there is a growing feeling, even among some Protestants, that the road forward leads South – and that the journey began with last December's meeting between Mrs Thatcher and the Irish Prime Minister.

Changing mood in the South

160 But what is the feeling in the South? Although the politicians there are well aware of the problem of administering a hostile population of one million Protestants, opinion polls there show that most people favour unity of some kind. A 1979 survey, for instance, showed that 41.2 per cent wanted unity under one govern-170 ment while 26.7 per cent wanted a federal Ireland.

The South knows it would have to make concessions (over the role of Catholic doctrine, for instance) in any talks on union. And, like their counterparts in the North, the politicians there do not want to surrender anything before they reach any negotiating table. But 180 there is a change of approach.

Instead of a simple "Brits Out" policy, Southerners are opening up a dialogue with the Unionists in the North.

But violence could disrupt any of the options

VIOLENCE, of course, could disrupt any of the options that are being discussed. All too often in 190 the past a carefully laid political strategy has been blown to pieces by one of the provisional IRA's more bloody initiatives.

Although Northern Ireland's security is better now than it has been for several years the price is high. True, the army is down to 10,840 soldiers, the lowest level since 1970; the army garrison has 200 only three infantry battalions on its gruelling four-month emergency tours, while the remainder are there for two-year tours of duty with their families, which leads to greater military stability.

But to compensate for this the police have once again had to become a paramilitary force. When it goes into republican areas 210 the RUC is armed like soldiers. In addition, the Ulster Defence Regiment, still seen by many Catho-lics as a sectarian band of armed Protestants, has had to be built up to a strength of 7,600.

The police maintain the rule of law, but it is in no sense normal law. Just one example: in 10 months from January of last year, 220 4,069 people were picked up under the emergency powers, but 85 per cent of them were never charged. The emergency laws are, according to one survey, being used for "screening, b u i l d i n g up dossiers, and harassment."

The role of the IRA

And none of this has defeated the IRA.

230 Their strength is only around 200 actively engaged in small service units with perhaps another 300 "civilians" behind them, but their equipment, like the new radio bombs, is increasingly sophisticated.

Provisional Sinn Fein Gerry Ad-290 ams, 32-year-old head of the organisation in the North

240 "You should ask the people of the 32 counties of Ireland if they wish the British to withdraw. The British government is here against the wishes of the Irish people and anything else after that becomes a distraction."

In the wake of the hungerstrikes recruitment has climbed dramatically, and in Derry they are turn-250 ing people away for the first time since Bloody Sunday in 1972. These new recruits will have been trained and armed in about six months, and there is evidence that their activities will be masterminded by provisionals from the North who see the Protestant community as much their enemy as is the British government. Their 260 ultimate aim is not talks with the government but making the North so ungovernable that British withdrawal becomes inevitable.

Neither violence nor the Provisionals fade away

The prospect of a fresh upsurge in violence bodes ill for the economy of the province, which is in a truly awful state, costing Britain £ 1.5 270 billion a year, and deteriorating rapidly. And this, too, helps to undermine the prospect of a successful new initiative.

The truth is that neither violence, nor the Provisionals, are going to fade away.

Their campaign to drive the British out by force will continue for the foreseeable future; and if that 280 kind of thinking dictates the pace of future events, then truly the prospects are bleak.

More support for a bold solution now

At most the violence is an excuse for inaction rather than an insuperable barrier to progress. If the British government had the will to contemplate a bold proposal now 290 for Northern Ireland, then it might, as our reports suggest, find far more support than it may have expected.

The groups opposing new solutions are familiar and definable. But perhaps they are not as formidable as they would like to pretend. There are many people in Northern Ireland who would like 300 to see them finally challenged.

(The Sunday Times, June 28, 1981)

Notes on the text:

William E. Gladstone, Liberal British Prime Minister between 1867 and 1894, tried to solve the Irish problem by reforms of the High Church (disestablishment) and land laws, and by introducing **Home** **Rule** (autonomy) for Ireland. These attempts failed, however, forcing his government to retreat and leaving the Liberals split.

What you have to do

Is there a way to an acceptable solution in Northern Ireland now?

The results of an Opinion Poll and a special report published by the SUNDAY TIMES in June 1981 provide a comprehensive and balanced assessment of the present situation in Northern Ireland. Use this information for your discussion in class.

Take the following points as a guide line.

1. Why are two of the six options unacceptable to a large majority among both communities?
2. Why won't the Protestant community accept two other options?
3. Another option is rejected by a majority of the Catholic community. Why?
4. The sixth option has a two-third majority support across sectarian lines. Why does a minority of each community, however, reject this solution?
5. There is a long way from a broad statistical consensus to a political strategy for a solution. What obstacles does the British government have to overcome, which groups might oppose or even fight a solution?

Prepare short introductory statements on these five points for your discussion in class. It's up to you whether you refer to all of the six options of the poll (p. 107) or concentrate on the most important.

Comprehension Piece

The releasing of Northern Ireland

THE BRITISH PRESENCE in Northern Ireland has become part of the problem rather than part of the solution. It was from that starting point that in a leader last week we advocated a British renunciation of sovereignty over the province, and its establishment as an independent state. Our case was that this would give both sides the essence of what they want: Catholics would be delivered from British rule, Protestants from the fear of Irish rule.

Here is a place where over 2,000 lives have been avoidably lost; where many thousands more have been ruined by bereavement and mutilation (and there the sufferers, after military casualties, are plentiful in Britain, too); where a whole generation of children has grown up in profoundly maiming conditions exposed to all the hurt and corruption of a state of suppressed war. Nothing of this is on the way to cure. The Thatcher administration, like its three predecessors, is barren of ideas. It is 10 years since that famous cry appeared on a wall in Ballymurphy – "Is there a life *before* death?" For the young people of Northern Ireland the answer is as dusty as ever.

Of course independence is an imperfect solution. The larger, not the smaller, unit is in idealistic terms the more appealing; the North-South border dissolved in some grander grouping – a British Isles Federation, a United States of Europe. But those hopes are not

111

for today's world. Again, coalition rule within the United Kingdom would have been an entirely sensible outcome; but that crashed when the Sunningdale settlement (cf. chronolgy, p. 115, Dec. 1973) did in 1974, and has looked increasingly unattainable since. The reality is that constitutional links between Britain and Ireland have been tried in many forms over many centuries, and have all failed. The task is now to find a framework which removes that cause of strife without substituting another.

We are told that to renounce sovereignty would be to encourage terrorism. Yet the British government cannot forswear good ideas simply because they are also backed by bad men. Further, it has to face the uncomfortable fact that historically and actually the presence of British troops is in itself an encouragement to terrorism. It was so after the First World War; it has been so again since 1971. The rise of the Provisional IRA was as much as anything else a reaction to British soldiers on the streets of Belfast.

A more pointed form of the same objection is that the Provisionals would press on from Northern independence to seek unity with the South. The experience of the Republic is that a native administration can take a much rougher line with Irish gunmen, and get away with it, than a British one can. More than that, though, real doubt surrounds the question of whether there would be continuing support for such a unity campaign, North or South. Although the ostensible aim of the Provisionals is an all-Ireland socialist republic, few of their sympathisers would follow them that far. The root Catholic instinct in the North is a rejection of British rule: nothing else.

Then there is the argument from the risk of widespread bloodshed. That is the threat which has paralysed British impulses to radicalism throughout this century. Sooner or later it must be shown to be surmountable. British troops will still be there when the British declaration of intent is made, and while the subsequent constitutional conference sits, and until the new state begins life. The risk is containable. And against this hypothetical damage must always be set the actual damage being inflicted on the people of Northern Ireland while inertia persists.

It goes without saying that an independent Northern Ireland presents problems.

The chief question is how to guard against the re-establishment of a Protestant-supremacist state.

The honest answer is that, if intelligent self-interest will not, no constitutional device can do the job irreversibly. Certainly Britain cannot. The last great service Britain can do for Northern Ireland is to leave it; and once power has been resigned it cannot be taken back from time to time to make adjustments.

Britain would not hand over power until Northern Ireland's representatives had agreed a written constitution with entrenched rights for the minority.

The Northern Irish are a peculiarly gifted people, highly politicised at all levels, well able to conduct their own affairs, with deep reserves of tenacity and courage. How else could they have stood what they have? It is all the more tragic that they should be doomed by Britain's inattentive presence to go on wasting their time and energies addressing the wrong problems.

The truth which the events of the past few months have made evident beyond denial is that the present state of affairs in Northern Ireland is indefensible. For Britain to pretend anything else any longer is a dereliction of the responsibilities of government.

(The Sunday Times, August 23, 1981, abridged)

Work sheet: "The releasing of Northern Ireland"

Questions on the text

Read all the questions first and plan your answers carefully in order to avoid repeating yourself. Use your own words as far as possible.

1. Which solutions to the problem in Northern Ireland are referred to in the text and which option does the author suggest?
2. Summarize in about 100 words the objections to the option suggested and the author's counterarguments.
3. Sum up the author's criticism of the Northern Ireland policies of British Governments since 1968 when the troubles began.

4. What is the explicit message of the writing on a wall in Ballymurphy "Is there a life before death?" (l.32)?
5. Rewrite the following two passages from the text without using the words in italics:
   - a whole generation of children has grown up . . . *exposed to* all the *hurt* and *corruption* of a state of *suppressed* war. (l.24-26)
   - the events of the past few months have *made evident beyond* denial that the present *state of affairs* in Northern Ireland is *indefensible*. (l.146-149)

The games children play reflect the realities of everyday conflict in Belfast.

Comment

1. In 1976 (cf p. 101 f.) the Sunday Times published the article "Why we should leave Ulster". Why was this headline not used again in this leader in August 1981? Comment on the implications of these two headlines.
2. Comment on the apparent contradiction between the results of the Sunday Times public opinion poll in June 1981 and the option suggested in this leader two months later.

Composition

Write a letter to the editor (about 200 words).

Give your view of the solution suggested and the arguments put forward in support of it. You may write from your personal point of view or a Republican, a Protestant Unionist or British standpoint.

Extra material

"800 years of Anglo-Irish history" – chronology

	The British Side	The Irish Side
1171	**Henry II,** Anglo-Norman king sends troops to Ireland. Becomes titular lord of Ireland.	Many Irish noblemen (Gaelic chiefs and landlords) lose their land. Anglo-Norman earldoms and baronages are set up.
16th – 17th century	Tudor and Stuart kings and queens of England conquer parts of Ireland and have them **colonized** by settlers.	Irish noblemen and landlords are supported by foreign enemies of England: esp. the Spanish fleet. Many of them have to leave the country.
1649	**Cromwell's** "anti Catholic crusades". Conquers the whole of Ireland and confiscates land for his supporters and veterans.	Catholic Irish aristocracy supports Charles II (later king of England). Cromwell removes most of them.
1690	William of Orange defeats Catholic James II **(Battle of the Boyne).** Confirms Protestant supremacy in Ireland.	Native Catholics (Irish and English) support James II.
End of 17th century		Most of the land of Ireland is owned by Protestants of English and Scottish origin.
18th century (2nd half)		**"Penal Code"** discriminates against Catholic (Irish) landlords and citizens.
1798		**United Irishmen** (coalition of Irish nationalists, Catholic and Protestant middle class Republicans stage rebellion against England. They are supported by French revolutionary forces.
1800	British Government under Conservative Prime Minister **Pitt** ties Ireland firmly to the **United Kingdom** of England, Scotland, Wales and – now – Ireland **("Act of Union").**	Protestant Irish **"Orange Order"** is founded in support of the political union with Great Britain.
1829	Westminster repeals Test Act: **Catholic Emancipation.**	Irish Catholics demand **Repeal** of the **Act of Union**
1886/92	British Prime Minister **W. E. Gladstone** introduces **Home Rule** bills (autonomy) for Ireland	

	The British Side	The Irish Side
1916.	British Government (Prime Minister **Asquith**) in trouble: World War I, foreign enemies (Germany) help Irish Nationalist movement.	Dublin 1916: **Easter Rising.** Organized by the Irish Republican Brotherhood (a militant group of the Nationalist movement). The Rising was immediately crushed by British troops.
1918		Overall majority of Nationalist forces (Sinn Fein and Nationalist Party) in general elections – except for the province of Ulster.
1919 – 21	British Government has to fight militant Irish Nationalist and Republican forces ("War of Independence" against British rule).	
1920	**Partition** of Northern Ireland (Ulster) and Southern Ireland (Eire) by British Government **(Lloyd George).**	Continued confrontation of **Unionist** (Protestant) and **Nationalist** (Catholic) groups in Northern Ireland.
Autumn 1968		**Civil Rights Movement** starts peaceful rallies and demonstrations in Ulster. Start of Derry and Belfast riots.
August 1969	British troops are sent to Northern Ireland.	
9. 8. 1971	British Government introduces **internment** in Northern Ireland.	300 people arrested (without trial).
30. 1. 1972		**Bloody Sunday** in Londonderry; 13 civilians shot by British troops during demonstration.
March 1972	British Government introduces **Direct Rule** in Northern Ireland.	Stormont (Ulster parliament) suspended.
December 1973	The British Government (Conserv.) presses through the Sunningdale power-sharing deal (named after the place of the conference): a local administration of N. I., with certain guaranteed powers for Catholics. Without being seriously tested this arrangement is given up after a Protestant general strike against it.	
2. 5. 1975		Northern Ireland Constitutional Convention elected. Unionists and militant Protestants obtain overall majority.
March 1976		Convention suspended without political results.

The British Side	The Irish Side
August 1976		**Peace Movement** rallies 20 000 people (mainly women and children) in demonstration for peace in Belfast.
October 1977		Nobel peace prize awarded to Women Peace Movement.
April 1978		The three leaders of the Peace Movement leave the executive council – there is no public support any longer.
March 30, 1979		The Irish National Liberation Army (INLA – a militant Republican faction that broke away from the official IRA in the mid-1970s after the official IRA had declared a ceasefire) claims responsibility for the murder of Airey Neave, Conservative MP, and shadow-N.I. Secretary, who was killed in the Houses of Parliament car park, at Westminster.
August 27, 1979		Lord Mountbatten, uncle of Prince Philip, the husband of Queen Elizabeth II, and three others killed in their fishing boat by a bomb planted by members of the INLA.
May and December 1980	Mrs Thatcher, British PM, and Mr Haughey, Irish PM, meet twice, at London and Dublin, for talks about N.I.'s future. Anglo-Irish "joint studies" begin.	
Throughout 1981		Hunger-strike movement in Northern Irish prisons by Republican prisoners: Bobby Sands, Republican hunger striker is elected Member of Parliament at Westminster for Sinn Fein in April 1981. Sands and three other hunger-strikers die in prison.
November 1985	**Anglo-Irish Agreement** between London and Dublin. The Republic of Ireland gives its most formal recognition ever that Ulster is part of the United Kingdom. In return Dublin gets a strong consultative role in the running of the province through a strengthened Anglo-Irish ministerial council.	

Latest statistics (March 20, 1988) put the death toll from "the troubles" in Northern Ireland at 2,645 since British troops moved in on August 14, 1969.

Glossary

Apprentice Boys: A Protestant and Loyalist organisation similar to the Orange Order. It commemorates 13 Protestant apprentices who shut the gates of Derry against the forces of the Catholic King James II during the great siege in 1688. Apprentice Boys from all over the North parade in Derry on 12 August each year. Membership usually overlaps with the Orange Order.

Black and Tans: Special forces recruited in England on a semi-mercenary basis to reinforce the Royal Irish Constabulary – much reduced by death and resignations – during the War of Independence. The Black and Tans were recruited largely from unemployed ex-service men and wore khaki uniforms with black police caps and belts – hence the name. They were brutal and undisciplined, served in Ireland from 1920 to 1922 and at the peak period there were 7000 Black and Tans in the country.

Dail (Eireann): The Parliament of Ireland since 1921

Fianna Fail (FF): Political party formed by de Valera in 1926 when he broke away from the Sinn Fein to enter the Free State Dail. Its policies were ostensibly mildly radical and Republican and most of the former Sinn Fein MPs joined it. The biggest party in the country and in the Dail. It has long since dropped any pretensions to radicalism or Republicanism however. In the EEC it aligns itself with the French Gaullist party.

Irish Citizen Army: Set up by James Larkin, the Labour leader, as a workers defence force after a great industrial struggle in Dublin in 1913. It took part with the Irish Volunteers in the 1916 Rising as well as in the War of Independence and on the Republican side in the Civil War but then disintegrated.

Irish Republican Army (IRA): The guerilla force which fought the War of Independence against the RIC and British Army 1919–21. The IRA split over the Treaty in 1922 with the pro-Treaty group becoming the army of the new Free State and the anti-Treaty group keeping the IRA title. They hid their weapons and continued to organise and train. De Valera and his followers split from them to enter the Dail in 1926 and members of their left wing left in the 1930s. The result was an underground organisation totally dedicated to ending partition by force and uninterested in "politics" The IRA carried out a bombing campaign in England in 1939–40 and two campaigns in the North, 1942–44 and 1956–62, all without success. In the mid – 1960s they moved to the left

and became involved in the Civil Rights movement in the North and social and economic agitation in the South. Frustration at this 'political' role and at the IRA's failure to defend the Catholic ghettos in August 1969 led to a further split, into the Provisional and Official IRA. The Officials favoured political action to reform Northern Ireland, the Provisionals a military campaign to destroy it.

Irish Republican Brotherhood (IRB): A revolutionary secret society dedicated to the establishment of an Irish Republic by force. It was first known as the Fenians and organised an unsuccesful rising in 1867, reorganised in 1873 and infiltrated the Sinn Fein party and the Irish Volunteers. It planned the 1916 Rising and reorganised the Volunteers into the IRA in 1918–1919. It supported the Treaty. The IRB ceased to have influence after 1922.

Irish Volunteers: A Nationalist force established in 1913 to counter the UVF already formed in the North. It was a faction of this force that staged together with Connolly's Citizen Army the 1916 Rising.

Orange Order: A politico-religious organisation dedicated to maintaining Protestant supremacy and the link with Britain No Catholic and no-one whose close relatives are Catholics may be a member. Founded in 1795 in Co. Armagh in 1795 during Catholic-Protestant clashes over land, it spread quickly, with some government encouragement, throughout Ulster and among Protestants in the rest of Ireland. The Orange Order declined in importance during the 19th century but revived in the 1880s when Home Rule became a serious possibility, and many prominent and respectable Unionists joined it. With its banners, sashes and parades and its fiercely anti-Catholic rhetoric it has been very effective in mobilising the Protestant masses in the Unionist cause. It has also frequently been the instrument of discrimination and patronage. The Orange Order is still strongly represented in the official Unionist Party.

Peoples Democracy (PD): Formed in Belfast in October 1968 as a leftist, student-based civil rights organisation and played a main role in the early Civil Rights campaign. It also played a major part in organising popular resistance in the Northern ghettos after the introduction of internment. The PD has been active in the South as well as against both Fianna Fail and Coalition governments.

Royal Irish Constabulary (RIC): The centrally-controlled Irish police force established in the 1830s and called the IRC in 1867. It was almost entirely Irish, mainly Catholic and about 1200 strong. It was disbanded in 1922.

Royal Ulster Constabulary (RUC): The new Northern Ireland police force established in 1922. Closely modelled on the RIC, it was also a centrally-controlled, armed, para-military force. It was recruited half from the old RIC, half from the Special Constabulary – themselves recruited from the UVF. It was always strongly Protestant and Unionist with Catholics only about 10 per cent of the total membership.

Sinn Fein: Founded in 1907 by Arthur Griffith as a separatist but not a Republican party. It was infiltrated by the IRB and after 1916 became the main voice of militant Republicanism, advocating abstention from the Westminster parliament and supporting the armed resistance of the IRA. Sinn Fein split over the Treaty in 1922, with the anti-Treaty majority keeping the title and adopting an abstentionist policy towards the new Free State parliament as well. De Valera and his supporters left in 1926 to set up Fianna Fail and enter the Dail and a group of left-wingers broke away in the 1930s to set up the Republican Congress.

From the 1930s on Sinn Fein has functioned mainly as the political wing of the IRA. In the 1960s it swung to the left in line with the IRA. In 1970 it split along the same lines as the IRA.

Social Democratic and Labour Party (SDLP): Set up in August 1970 by six opposition MPs at Stormont. 3 of them, Paddy Devlin, Gerry Fitt, and Austin Curry were members of existing parties. It has become the main opposition party in the North. It is now for power-sharing. It has become the voice of the Catholic middle class in the North. It supports social reforms.

Special Air Services Regiment (SAS): The SAS is a highly-secret crack unit of the British Army. Set up during the Second World War it has been used for plain-clothes, counter-insurgency and special operations work in a number of countries. After many denials Westminster finally admitted that SAS personnel were active in Northern Ireland.

Stormont: Parliament of Northern Ireland up to 1972

Ulster Defence Association (UDA): Hard-line Loyalist para-military group formed at the end of 1971 out of existing 'defence'-groups. The UDA is heavily armed and has been mainly responsible for the assassination campaign against Catholic civilians. The UDA is closely linked with the Vanguard Party.

Ulster Defence Regiment (UDR): A local part-time military force established in 1970 to replace the B-Specials. It was quickly infiltrated by the Loyalist para-military groups. It is now heavily armed and its strength is about 8000.

Ulster Special Constabulary (USC): The 'Specials' were an auxiliary para-military force raised in 1920 by the British. There were three categories: A (full-time), B (part-time), C (no regular duties). The A and C Specials were disbanded in 1925 but the 'B men' were mobilised during IRA campaigns. They were disbanded in 1969 as a result of civil rights protests.

Ulster Unionist Party: An Ulster Unionist Council separate from the Southern Irish Unionists was established in 1905, committed to opposing Home Rule and to keeping Ireland, and especially Ulster, within the United Kingdom! It had close lines with the Conservative Party and was dominated by industrialists, merchants and landowners. From the beginning the Orange Order was directly represented on the Council, which became the governing body of an Ulster Unionist Party. The party was and has remained the voice of the vast majority of Northern Protestants: it formed the government of the new six-county state in 1921 and remained in power until Stormont was suspended in 1972.

Ulster Volunteer Force (UVF): Established in 1913 by the Ulster Unionist Council as a private army to resist Home Rule. The UVF was re-formed in 1920 during the War of Independence and heavily involved in attacks on the Catholic population of the North over the next few years. It disappeared after 1922.

The UVF was revived by a small Loyalist group who murdered two Catholics in 1966. Since 1969 the UVF has expanded into a large paramiliatary organisation, more disciplined than the UDA but equally involved in sectarian killings. It has connections with the British National Front organisation.

United Irish League (UIL): Set up in 1898 as a mass organisation to agitate for land reform, the UIL helped to re-unite the divided Irish Home Rule Party. The UIL was effectively the voice of the Irish Catholic middle class and the Church before the First World War. After 1916 it was swept aside by Sinn Fein, in the North a little later.

United Irishmen: Founded in 1791 in Belfast, the United Irishmen was a revolutionary democratic society inspired by the French Revolution and dedicated to establishing an independent democratic Republic in Ireland.

Vanguard Unionist Progressive Party (VUPP): Founded by William Craig in February 1972 as an umbrella organisation for Loyalist parliamentarians and para-military groups, generally called Ulster Vanguard. It held a series of rallies early in 1792 with Craig reviewing men in military formation and crowds giving him the Fascist salute. In March 1973 Vanguard became a formal political party with Craig as leader.

Ulster Politicians

Craig, William: Leader of the Vanguard Unionist Party (VUPP), until very recently next to Paisley and West one of the hard-liners among the Protestant leaders in the Northern Ireland

Fitt, Gerry: One of the leading politicians in the Social Democratic And Labour Party (SDLP)

Faulkner, Brian: Unionist leader and up to 1969 Prime Minister of Northern Ireland, moderate in his policy towards the Catholics. He died in March 1977.

Paisley, Rev. Ian: Most widely known Protestant leader in Northern Ireland, one of the Protestant extremists, founded the Democratic Unionist Party, a loyalist party of the extreme right (1971). The DUP is closely associated with the Free Presbyterian Church, a breakaway fundamentalist Protestant church founded in 1951 of which he is the permanent Moderator or Head.

West, Harry: Leader of the official Unionist Party, another hardliner among the Protestant Ulster politicians.

References

1. Books

Comerford, Anthony, (ed.) — The Easter Rising: Dublin 1916, London 1969 (Jackdaw 61)

The Concise Oxford Dictionary of Current English — ed. by Sykes, J. B. Oxford 1976

de Paor, Liam — Divided Ulster, Harmondsworth et al. ²1973 "The best short summary of the Ulster problem so far" (Guardian)

Edwards, Ruth Dudley — An Atlas of Irish History, London 1973

Disturbances in Northern Ireland — Report of the Commission appointed by the Governor of Northern Ireland (Cameron Report), Belfast, HMSO September 1969 Cmd. 532

Farrell, Michael — Northern Ireland: The Orange State, London 1976 "The book is marvellously researched and packed with detail which is never allowed to swamp the racy narrative" Derek Brown, Guardian, 13/5/1976

Heffner, Richard D. — A Documentary History of the United States, London et al. 1975

Kennelly, Brendan — Selected Poems, Dublin 1969

–, (ed.) — The Penguin Book of Irish Verse, Harmondsworth et al. 1974

Limpkin, Clive — The Battle of Bogside, Harmondsworth et al., 1972

O'Connor, Ulick (ed.) — Irish Liberation, New York 1975

The People's Bicentennial Commission (ed.) — Voices of the American Revolution New York 1975

Woodham-Smith, Cecil — The Great Hunger – Ireland 1845–49, London 1974

2. Newspaper articles quoted from:

Claxton, Carol M.
"Background to the Troubles. A short history of Ireland in 2 parts. From: World and Press, Aug./Sept. 1976

Holland, Mary
"How the IRA gained a Sniper" From: The Observer, 6/2/1972

Leader article
"The releasing of Northern Ireland" From: The Sunday Times, 23/8/1981

Lipsey, David et. al.
"Is there another way?" Opinion poll and special report. From: The Sunday Times, 8/6/1981

Mirror Comment
"Ulster, Bloody Ulster" From: The Daily Mirror, 7/1/1976

Neave, Airey
"A speech on Ulster" From: The Sunday Times, 21/11/1976

Ryder, Chris
"What 7 years of violence have done to Alcwyn McKee" From: The Sunday Times, 29/8/1976

Statistics
From: The Sunday Times, 11/1/1976

Stephens, Robert & Yates, Ivan
"Who is Fighting Whom? What is the Fight about?" From: The Observer, 6/2/1972

Whale, John
"The End of a Long Story in Ireland" From: The Sunday Times, 13/1/1974
"Why we should leave Ulster" From: The Sunday Times, 30/10/1976

3. Poems

Kennelly, Brendan "My Dark Fathers";
Yeats, William Butler "Easter 1916" from: Irish Liberation, loc. cit.

4. Visual material

Photograph (p. 12) from: C. Limpkin, The Battle of Bogside, Harmondsworth 1972; Cartoon (p. 14) from: (H. Vogt, Konfessionskrieg in Nordirland, Stuttgart–München 1973; Photographs (p. 15) from: C. Limpkin, loc. cit.; Photographs (p. 16) from: The Sunday Times, 29/8/1976; Maps of Belfast (p. 16) from: M. Farrell, Northern Ireland: The Orange State, London 1976; Cartoon "Putting the clock back" (p. 28) from: The Observer, 19/1/1975; Portrait Elizabeth I. (p. 34) from: British Features, Bonn o. J.; Portrait James I. (p. 34) from: Jackdaw 53, London 1968; Portrait Cromwell (p. 35) from: Jackdaw 27, London 1966; Portrait William of Orange (p. 36) from Newsweek, 3/4/1972; Drawing Liberty Bell 1776 (p. 40) from: The Voices of the American Revolution, New York 1975; Portrait Pitt the Younger (p. 41) from: The American Peoples Encyclopedia Vol. 15, New York 1966; Illustrations (p. 48) from: Jackdaw 61, London 1969; Illustration (p. 51) from: Irish Liberation, loc. cit.; Drawing The Plough and the Stars (p. 53) from: Jackdaw 61, loc. cit.; Photographs (p. 55) from: Jackdaw 61, loc. cit.; Poster (p. 59) from: Jackdaw 61, loc. cit.; Illustration (p. 60) from: Irish Liberation, loc. cit.; Map of Londonderry (p. 62) from: Cameron Report, loc. cit.; Photograph (p. 72) from: Record cover "Songs of Irish Civil Rights" Mailand 1973; Photograph (p. 78) from: b:e Feb. 1977; Graph (p. 80 and 84) from: The Sunday Times 11/1/1976; Cartoon (p. 82) from: The Observer 6/2/1972; Cartoon (p. 96) from: The Sunday Times 11/1/1976. Cartoon (p. 109) from: The Times 9/12/1980. Photograph (p. 110) from: The Sunday Times 28/6/1981. Photograph (p. 113) from: Camerawork No. 14, London 1979.